Taking Stock

Taking Stock

Employee Ownership at Work

Michael Quarrey, Joseph Blasi, and Corey Rosen

■■

Ballinger Publishing Company
Cambridge, Massachusetts
A Subsidiary of Harper & Row, Publishers, Inc.

International Standard Book Number: 0-88730-131-2

Library of Congress Catalog Card Number: 86-14045

Printed in the United States of America

Library of Congress Cataloging-in-Publication Data

Quarrey, Michael.
  Taking stock.

  Bibliography: p.
  Includes index.
  1. Employee ownership—United States. 2. Employee stock ownership plans—United States. 3. Job satisfaction—United States. I. Blasi, Joseph R. II. Rosen, Corey M. III. Title.
HD5660.U5Q37 1986   338.7'4   86-14045
ISBN 0-88730-131-2

CONTENTS

v

PREFACE

For most of our industrial history, a good job meant a job that was safe, secure, and well paid. A good worker was an employee who was competent, reliable, and cooperative. The massive U.S. market was relatively undisturbed by foreign competition and, except for periodic disruptions, the economy provided a level of prosperity most other nations could only envy.

We are in a very different time today. Companies and industries undreamed of a few decades ago are emerging, while many basic U.S. industries are struggling or disappearing. New technologies are demanding new ways to work. A more educated and mobile workforce seeks more from work, and companies ask more from workers. The result has been an almost frantic search for new ways to organize jobs and companies. Business books, once relegated to the back shelves of bookstores, are suddenly nationwide bestsellers. Managers and workers alike are experts on theories from x to y to z, from "just-in-time" management to "management by walking around." As *Inc.* magazine aptly put it, "workstyle" is an increasingly central issue for U.S. business.[1]

While many of these developments are merely fads or cosmetic, there is little doubt that some very real and significant changes are occurring. Perhaps none of these is as potentially sweeping as employee ownership. While employee ownership plans were created by the federal government for the main statutory purpose of broadening the distribution of the ownership of wealth, they nonetheless have the potential to serve as the underpinning of some of the most innovative and promising ways to make work more rewarding, productive, and fulfilling.

Employee ownership has had a long history in the United

States, but it has gained a secure and broad foothold in the American economy only in the last decade. Over 8,000 firms with more than 11 million workers now have employee ownership plans. We estimate that most of these workers are in companies with less than 15 percent employee ownership. About one million workers are in companies that are 15 to 50 percent employee owned, and there are about 1,000 firms with 51 to 100 percent ownership by about 500,000 workers.

The plans vary tremendously, but they all share a common purpose: providing a capital ownership stake for workers. Realizing that too few people own too much capital, Congress has passed more than fifteen laws since 1974 to encourage companies to set up employee ownership plans. A more equitable distribution of ownership, Congress has contended, would not only be more fair but would also help millions of Americans realize their dreams of starting a business, educating their children, providing for their retirement, or otherwise pursuing ambitions that only more substantial financial resources can provide.

A substantial number of employee ownership companies are now moving beyond this central purpose of employee ownership to involve their employee-owners in the management of their jobs and even their companies. The results are often exciting and always instructive. This book focuses on fifteen of the most progressive cases of employee ownership at work.

Changing Work

Employee ownership is but one of many efforts now underway to change work. While we believe that it is also the most important, it is useful to place employee ownership in the context of other such efforts.

In 1982 the New York Stock Exchange published one of the first estimates of how many U.S. corporations were experimenting with human resource programs.[2] Of the 49,000 companies they studied, about 14 percent had developed programs. Most of these firms were motivated by a desire to cut costs, improve employee morale, follow the example of other corporations, increase productivity, or change their management philosophy.

The programs were of all types, ranging from job enlargement and rotation to improved training and feedback, to suggestion systems, labor/management committees, quality circles, and a variety of financial incentives (see Table 1). Some of the most innovative companies were cutting the number of reporting levels; cross-utilizing employees in different jobs; blurring lines of authority, communication, and responsibility; and otherwise escaping from the rigid constraints of an organizational chart. Seventy percent of the companies with over 500 employees were trying to involve workers in decisionmaking in some way, and only 3 percent of the managers interviewed believed that participative management was just a passing fad. Many of the companies had some form of gainsharing plan such as piecework (10%), group productivity incentives (7%), profit sharing (25%), and stock purchase plans (21%). The study did not, however, report on the most common types of employee ownership.

Changing some aspect of the job or acting on more employee suggestions in various ways are the predominant kinds of experiments. Programs that give workers a good deal of autonomy—labor-management committees, labor-advisory groups, production teams, task forces, and financial incentives—are not receiving as much attention. The exception is quality circles, where responsibility is often limited. Companies with employee ownership were almost four times more likely to have human resource programs. Obviously, employee ownership companies with progressive attitudes toward human resources merit a closer look.

How can we evaluate employee ownership within this broad context of the economic challenges and organizational changes the U.S. workplace has witnessed in the last decade? Why should we focus on employee ownership, and by what standards should we judge it?

Table 1. Percentage of Corporations Having Specified Activity

Activities	Employment Size					NYSE-Listed	Manufacturing		All Non-Manufacturing
	Total	500-999	1,000-4,999	5,000-24,999	25,000+		All	10,000+ Employees	
Job design/redesign	46%	51%	39%	47%	56%	42%	50%	45%	42%
Job enlargement	22	22	15	30	34	25	21	29	23
Job rotation	18	14	16	23	38	25	16	31	21
Formal training & instruction	76	75	68	87	89	82	74	87	78
Setting employee goals	64	58	66	74	68	67	59	69	70
Employee appraisal & feedback	72	62	79	82	75	75	67	71	77
Setting company objectives	55	54	54	55	57	58	49	55	61
Structuring plant & office space	29	43	15	34	17	22	34	23	23
Organizational structure	40	36	42	45	44	42	41	49	39
Scheduling work flow	43	46	37	49	41	41	40	39	46

Personalized work hours	28	35	20	21	41	27	24	30	33
Suggestion systems	38	29	36	54	56	48	34	57	44
Labor/management committees	25	30	17	27	30	26	34	36	14
Labor advisory groups	6	8	4	5	8	4	8	5	4
Quality circles	44	43	29	66	65	55	58	75	27
Production teams	16	12	12	28	32	26	23	41	9
Salarying blue collar workers	6	6	3	12	12	6	9	14	3
Task forces	35	31	30	42	50	40	37	42	32
Surveys of employee attitudes	45	33	42	64	70	57	43	61	47
Financial Incentives									
Piecework	10	9	6	17	15	14	14	20	4
Group productivity	7	8	4	9	16	9	6	11	9
Profit sharing	25	30	19	31	18	22	23	19	27
Stock purchase plans	21	17	22	27	23	33	26	27	16

Source: New York Stock Exchange, 1982.

A Critical Approach

Most of the recent workplace reforms are piecemeal—a company will try profit sharing or quality of worklife, a productivity plan or fewer levels of management, or perhaps combine two or three of these approaches. But few companies are ready to address the basic relationship between work, ownership, and management; to seek a new workplace in which workers participate in both corporate growth and decisionmaking at many levels. By contrast, the fifteen companies highlighted in this book not only have significant employee ownership plans but generally have both profit sharing and active employee involvement as well. In many ways they are on the cutting edge of the trends in rethinking work.

What are some key points to keep in mind while taking a critical look at employee ownership nationally and in these fifteen companies? First, we need to look at the various plans in terms of the financial rewards they provide to employees. This, after all, is the principal goal of employee ownership legislation. We should also consider employee ownership in terms of how it is restructuring work itself. In this respect, employee ownership can be evaluated in at least three other contexts: the separation of ownership and working; the relationship between ownership and productivity; and the connection between ownership and enjoying a job.

The Financial Rewards of Ownership

Does employee ownership significantly broaden the ownership of wealth? Again, we emphasize, this is the central purpose of employee ownership legislation and a chief criterion for evaluating its success or failure. Employee ownership plans should be providing their participants with real capital estates.

This is essentially a long-term benefit, and in many cases it may be substantial. Nevertheless, an employee ownership program should not be confused with a retirement plan since there is risk in investing primarily in a single company. To reduce these risks, employee ownership companies may have separate diversified pension plans, or they may take other steps to ensure that employees have or prepare for a secure retirement income. Unfortunately, we lack sufficient data to know to what, if any, extent companies are substituting employee ownership plans for traditional, diversified pension plans.

Some employee ownership companies also provide important short-term financial benefits. They may have profit-sharing plans, pay dividends, or have incentive programs to give employees a more immediate financial reward for their contribution to corporate performance.

The Separation of Ownership and Working

The idea that people should own their work—own their tools, their land, their shops—is not new in the United States. Some of the first settlers who came here, and the generations of immigrants who followed them, came pursuing this idea. This American dream of broad ownership of wealth made possible our experiment in political democracy and helped transform our economy.

With the rise of the large industrial corporation, however, ownership has concentrated into fewer and fewer hands. Aside from questions about the fairness of such a distribution, many argue that something more, something intangible, has been lost —that the American dream of owning one's own job has faded.

This separation of ownership and working does not have the rule of law, or even the superiority of tradition in the United States. In fact, the country has just recently gotten used to it. Until this century, a much larger proportion of the population actually worked more cooperatively in family units or near the home. Family-owned businesses are the remnant of that lifestyle.

Does employee ownership hold the promise of reviving that dream? Is it intrinsically more satisfying to be a worker sharing the risks and benefits of ownership? Can employee ownership recapture a lost familylike quality in American business?

Ownership and Productivity

The relationship between employee ownership and corporate performance has received considerable attention in recent years. It is a common-sense notion that when workers have a direct stake in the profitability of their company they will work harder and smarter. But to date no study has definitively established an automatic link between employee ownership and improved corporate performance.

Productivity studies show that people account for 50 percent of the controllable costs in production enterprises and 85 percent in labor-intensive service companies.[3] If employee ownership can tap the creative potential and problem-solving skills of workers, it has great potential for increasing productivity. Cost savings in employee ownership firms may also result from lowering supervisory expenses and even eliminating entire levels of management because of increased worker commitment.

The importance of employee ownership for productivity improvement is now more fully appreciated because of the failure of quality circle programs in some companies. Unions in particular have resisted quality circles because, they argue, workers do not want a vague sense of increased involvement, but real access to the economic rewards of increased output. Properly structured incentives comprised of employee ownership and profit sharing may offer a new direction for improving productivity.

Ownership and Job Satisfaction

Finally, owning the workplace and participating in decisionmaking does not necessarily make any job a good job. Many jobs are boring and cut off from human contact; most have little latitude for inventiveness and meaning. People may like their company, like the people they work with, like being employee owners, and still hate their work.

Employee ownership cannot be expected to magically eliminate all expressions of disinterest on the part of employees:

absenteeism; lack of initiative; inefficiency; carelessness; and feelings of alienation and hostility. Nor can it be expected, in itself, to do away with management's disinterest: poor working conditions; ineffective supervision; lack of attention to health and safety; inflexible fringe benefits; inability to recognize employee achievements. But can it be the basis for addressing these problems? Does the fact that workers are owners give them more power to reshape and improve their jobs? Does it encourage managers to treat their employees better? Does it provide employees with more incentive to respond to greater opportunities on their jobs?

To make a job more interesting a company can expand the number and variety of tasks its employees complete. It can enrich jobs by providing more opportunity for workers to plan and control their work. Workers can be given responsibility for such things as scheduling and ordering supplies, or they can learn each others' skills and rotate jobs. Autonomous work teams can function as supportive social groups that also perform quality control through peer pressure.

Ultimately, it is clear that we may not be able to structure all jobs to make them more satisfying. This would obviously be an unrealistic expectation of employee ownership. Still, employee ownership companies could do much to improve individual jobs and the general environment and conditions surrounding jobs.

Characteristics of the Fifteen Companies

With this framework for analysis in mind, let's take a look at the fifteen companies in this book. Table 2 outlines the major characteristics of the companies. They are in a variety of businesses all over the country. M. W. Carr, a Massachusetts-based light manufacturer, makes picture frames, while Hyatt-Clark manufactures ball bearings in New Jersey for the automobile industry. ERC is a high technology professional services company in California. Western Airlines and the Lowe's Companies are large public companies spread out over wide geographic areas.

Table 2. Company Characteristics

Company	Principal Product/Industry	Public/ Private	# Emp.	Union	Plan Type	Reason	% Owned	Vote	Part. Grps	Board Reps.
M.W. Carr	mfg. picture frames	private	250	no	ESOP	incentive	100	yes	yes	yes
ERC	prof. services	public	650	no	ESOP DP	start-up	19 43	yes	yes	yes
Quad/ Graphics	gravure printing	private	2,000	no	ESOP	philosophy	37	no	yes	no
Phillips Paper Corp.	dist. packaging products	private	42	no	DP PS ESOP	philosophy/ incentive	20	yes	yes	yes
Hyatt-Clark Industries	mfg. automotive ball bearings	private	1,500	yes	ESOP	buyout	100	no	yes	yes
Solar Center	manufacturer and installation solar hot water heaters	private	25	no	COOP ESOP	start-up	100	yes	yes	yes
Allied Plywood Corp.	wholesale distributor plywood	private	30	no	ESOP	family transfer	100	yes	no	yes
Fastener Industries	mfg. industrial weld fasteners	private	125	no	ESOP	family transfer	100	yes	yes	yes

Company	Business	Public/Private		Plan	Reason	%			
Up-Right, Inc.	mfg. metal staging	public	780 no	PS ESOP	benefit/philosophy	40	yes	no	no
Western Airlines	commuter passenger airline	public	10,500 yes	ESOP	stock for wages	32	no	no	yes
Workers' Owned Sewing	garment sewing	private	70 no	COOP	create jobs (economic development)	100	yes	yes	yes
Lowe's Companies	retail home centers	public	8,000 no	ESOP	benefit/incentive	30	yes	no	no
Once Again Nut Butter	manufacturing & distribution natural peanut butter	private	5 no	COOP	experiment	100	yes	yes	yes
Common Ground	restaurant	private	23 no	COOP	philosophy	100	yes	yes	yes
Freewheel Bicycle	bike shop	private	40 no	COOP	philosophy	100	yes	yes	yes

Note:
ESOP —employee stock ownership plan;
COOP —worker cooperative;
DP —direct stock purchase plan;
PS —profit-sharing plan that invests in company stock.

There is a magazine printer in Wisconsin, a Vermont restaurant, a Minneapolis bike shop, a Virginia plywood distributor, a Berkely scaffolding manufacturer, and a North Carolina garment-sewing company.

The companies are of all different sizes. Once Again Nut Butter has only 5 employees; Western Airlines has over 10,000. Most of the companies, like most employee ownership companies, are private, and only two of them have unions.

Eleven of the companies have employee stock ownership plans, or ESOPs, the most common form of employee ownership. The other four companies are worker cooperatives. The companies typify the broad range of reasons for setting up employee ownership plans. Some, like San Francisco's Solar Center, simply have a philosophical commitment to the concept; others, such as Lowe's, have adopted it as an employee benefit or incentive. Still others have used employee ownership as a means to transfer ownership from retiring owners (Allied Plywood), as an economic development tool (Workers' Owned Sewing), and, in one case, as a way to save jobs that would have been lost had a plant been forced to close (Hyatt-Clark).

Our observations of nationwide trends indicate that the transfer of businesses to employees by retiring owners accounts for more than 60 percent of the new sizably or majority employee-owned companies. And, contrary to popular belief, employee ownership has been used to save failing companies only in an extremely small number of cases. Fewer than 100 of the estimated 1,000 majority employee-owned companies are such distress buyouts.

Each company is providing a significant ownership share to its employees, ranging from 20 to 100 pecent of the outstanding equity. Many of the companies also have profit sharing or incentive programs to provide short-term benefits, and Up-Right has developed an unusual way to protect ESOP benefits from declining stock values.

Some companies have gone further than others with employee participation, and most have changed their participation programs as they have gained experience. The mechanisms the companies use vary widely and include voting rights on shares, job-level participation groups, representation on the board, and other approaches.

In each of the fifteen companies the structure of the employee ownership plan and participation program is the unique outcome of a specific corporate history; and each company continues to experiment and change. The companies have not been selected as a statistical cross section of employee ownership. Rather, they have been included more to suggest the various possibilities for creative and successful uses of employee ownership at work.

ACKNOWLEDGMENTS

Many of the companies in this book were studied by the National Center for Employee Ownership under a research grant from the National Institute for Mental Health. We are appreciative of the financial support of NIMH and are particularly grateful to Richard Wakefield and Elliot Liebow for their guidance through the grant application process. We would also like to thank Katherine Klein, who gathered and analyzed most of the data during the three-year project, and Karen Young, who administered the grant.

The National Cooperative Bank in Washington, D.C. also provided financial support for the book. The book owes much to the helpfulness of NCB's Geoffrey Caldwell and Stephanie Hevenstein, and to the generosity of the bank.

In addition to NCEO staff, a number of students and faculty gathered information on the companies in the book, including: Andy Lisak (Common Ground, Freewheel, and Quad/Graphics); Megan Campbell (M. W. Carr); Michael Caudell-Feagan (Lowe's); Ramona Ford (Phillips Paper); Keith Kirkpatrick (Phillips Paper); Allison Read (Solar Center); Gail Sokoloff (Hyatt-Clark); Sergio Storch (M. W. Carr); and Bryan Wilson (Hyatt-Clark). Joseph Blasi wishes to thank William Foote Whyte, David Bloom, Philip Warburg, and Kathy Cahill for their assistance.

Karen Young, Lisa Gilman, Ira Wagner, Matthew Trachman, and Sam Wessinger all provided thoughtful criticism of the manuscript as did the staff at Ballinger, including Marjorie Richman, Lynn Schroeder, and Barbara Roth. We are also grateful to Margaret Schnoor, who did most of the final typing, as well as Willa Seidenberg for her efforts in typing and proofreading.

Most of all, of course, we want to thank the companies and their employees for participating in the studies, and, more important, for providing such excellent examples of employee ownership at work.

1

INTRODUCTION

T en years ago only a handful of U.S. businesses offered their employees a significant share of ownership in their company. Today you could get dressed in clothes made by Blue Bell's Wrangler division, eat a breakfast of Starflower Granola, sweeten your coffee with sugar from U.S. Sugar, fly from New York to Los Angeles on People Express, while the flight away reading any of several major magazines printed by Quad/Graphics, catch a United Taxi (Los Angeles' biggest cab company) at the L.A. airport, cook a dinner using the Moosewood Cookbook from the Moosewood Restaurant, and fall asleep under a Bates' Fabric George Washington bedspread (the nation's most popular). Everyone of these companies is at least 25 percent employee owned. They are just a few of the over 8,000 companies that are at least partly employee owned —companies that now employ 7 to 8 percent of the workforce.

Employee ownership now lists hundreds of major firms among its ranks. For instance:

- The nation's most profitable steel company, Weirton Steel, is 100 percent employee owned, as is the 10,000-employee Avondale Industries (shipbuilding and other manufacturing);

- Science Applications (6,000 employees) and W. L. Gore Associates (3,000 employees) are just two among many fast-growing employee-owned high-tech firms;

- Employees have become major owners at several airlines, including, Western (32%), People Express (33%), Republic

(15%), TWA (20%), Southwest (15%), and America West (20%);

- In trucking, three of the nations's ten largest carriers (Ryder/P-I-E, Hall's and Smith's Transfer) are now at least 40 percent employee owned;

- Employees own 100 percent of retailing giants Pamida (5,000 employees) and OTASCO (3,000 employees);

- Employees are majority owners of Davey Tree, one of the nation's largest tree service firms (2,600 employees), Lifetouch Studios, a 4,000-employee photographic firm, and the 7,000-employee Parsons Engineering.

These are only a few examples. Employee ownership has in just a decade become established in every industry, in every region, in every size company. It is no longer just an intellectual curiosity or distant nostrum; it is part of the way we do business.

The growth of employee ownership is an important and intriguing example of how social change can be accomplished in the United States. This book surveys this phenomenon by presenting fifteen cases of employee ownership, cases that represent the broad spectrum of ways in which employee ownership is being used.

The Development of Employee Ownership in the United States

The idea of broadly owned capital is hardly new. People first came to the United States, at least in large part, because they wanted to own their own productive capital, which at that time meant owning land. The American colonies and later the American nation helped translate this yearning into reality by making land available to those willing to work it, and later, by helping develop arid lands for use by small farmers. This policy of broadened ownership was enormously successful, both as an economic and as a social experiment. The United States became the world's most prosperous nation and most long-lived democracy.

At least some of the founding fathers believed that the principles developed for land ownership should be extended to industry as well. Albert Gallatin, Secretary of the Treasury under Jefferson and Madison and one of the leading thinkers of his time, argued that "the democratic principle upon which this nation was founded should not be restricted to the political process but should be applied to the industrial operations as well."[1]

It didn't work out that way, of course. The industrial revolution brought with it a new kind of ownership—the limited liability corporation, with a class of owners, some of whom were managers, and a class of nonowning employees they hired. In unchecked form, it was an ownership situation that allowed, even demanded, the exploitation of workers. Eventually, labor laws and labor unions became a counterforce to this narrow ownership structure, providing workers with more security, better working conditions, and higher pay.

The system has worked fairly well for the last century, but not well enough. The adversarial relationship between workers and the representatives of owners (management) has prevented too many U.S. companies from taking full advantage of the human resources they have. We could afford underutilization when foreign competition was limited to a relatively small share of our market; we cannot afford it in an increasingly competitive global market. More importantly, the separation of work and ownership has created a widening gap between the wealthy and everyone else. Just 1 percent of the population owns over 50 percent of the privately held wealth in the United States, a distribution of wealth more skewed than that of virtually every other industrial Western nation.[2]

This inequity is more than a problem of justice. It is also a problem of missed opportunities. When more people are owners of capital, more people have the resources to start new businesses, to make major purchases, to educate their children, to move to more attractive jobs, to retrain, or otherwise to pursue their dreams. That's good for these people, and it is also good for the economy, for it maintains a dynamism and spirit essential for innovation, growth, and competition.

Broadened ownership is also essential if we are to resolve the tension between growth and equity that has characterized U.S. politics for the last several decades. On the one hand, conservatives tend to argue that we need policies that stimulate investment and thus growth. Growth, they maintain, is the best way to benefit everyone. Unfortunately, to stimulate investment, those with wealth to invest must be given incentives, which makes them even wealthier. Liberals contend this is inequitable and press for policies that redistribute wealth. The problem, of course, has been that many of the programs to do this have not worked, and, even if they have had some success, they have often taken money out of private investment, thus slowing growth or fueling inflation. But what if capital were widely owned? Then policies that increased the return to capital would, by their nature, be more equitable. People would be more willing to accept proinvestment policies, while a whole new approach to creating social justice would become available—one that could use the market to help enrich the many rather than the few.

It was with these thoughts in the air that the current wave of interest in employee ownership began. Although there have been periodic spurts of interest in worker cooperatives and in management-initiated employee ownership programs, especially during the 1920s, it is only in the last decade that employee ownership has become institutionalized through government, corporate, and union policies, as well as through acceptance by the press, financial institutions, and academia as a legitimate subject of interest.[3] This is an important point. Previous waves of interest in employee ownership have been generated more by a desire for worker control, as in worker cooperatives, or finding a better way to bind employee interests to the company, as in the "New Capitalism" movement of the 1920s. While elements of both concerns can be found in the current interest in employee ownership, its base of support, and the source of its federal tax breaks, has been the desire to broaden the distribution of the ownership of wealth.

The Development of the ESOP

The key figures in generating this current interest in employee ownership have been Louis Kelso and Russell Long.[4] Building on the idea of stock bonus plans, which had been around for decades, Kelso created the ESOP—employee stock ownership plan. Essentially, an ESOP was a stock bonus plan that could borrow money (more on this later). Kelso also suggested a number of other "SOPs," such as consumer stock ownership plans, housing stock ownership plans, and so on, but it was the ESOP that caught on. Kelso argued that the problem with capitalism was that there were too few capitalists. Workers in particular were being deprived of the chance to earn income from capital, instead having to rely entirely on selling their labor to make a living. The result, Kelso contended, was that wages were forced up beyond what labor was really contibuting to production, but paradoxically, workers were still not getting rich enough. The reason was that capital ownership was far too narrowly held, meaning that a few people were capturing enormous wealth—more than they could ever spend. Kelso argued that this situation was not only inefficient but immoral, and he proposed the ESOP as a means to change it. By sharing ownership with workers, more people would own capital and companies would be more competitive.

At first Kelso sought to persuade companies to set up ESOPs, but he enjoyed only limited success. Existing laws were ambiguous on whether an ESOP would be able to qualify for the tax breaks Kelso said it would, and companies were reluctant to set up plans that might later be ruled illegal. In 1973 Kelso met with Senator Russell Long and the problem was solved. Long, son of populist Louisiana governor and senator Huey Long, agreed passionately that there were too few capitalists and that society had become inequitable. A generally conservative senator on most economic matters, he saw the ESOP as the ideal means by which the market system, not a government program, could be used to broaden the ownership of capital, and do it in a way that relied on a fairer distribution of newly created wealth rather than a redistribution of existing wealth.

Long took these arguments to Congress, where he succeeded in creating a favorable legislative framework for ESOPs, one that he enhanced with new legislation in virtually every succeeding Congress. By 1985 fifteen states had followed this congressional lead by passing laws of their own. With the help of these laws and a growing perception that employee ownership was a good idea, ESOPs and other employee ownership plans began to grow quickly, expanding from about 300 in 1973 to 8,000 today. While the laws are complex, they essentially make it in the financial self-interest of employers to share ownership with employees.

These new tax incentives came at the same time that changes in the workforce and the global economy were creating conditions ripe for changes in the organization of work. Workers were better educated than ever before, and many were looking for more from work than just a secure, well-paying job. Of course, these well-paying jobs had helped make the U.S. market a very attractive one, one that foreign competitors were penetrating more and more effectively. In the past U.S. companies could afford some inefficiency, but not any longer. If companies were to attract and keep the best workers, and if they were to use these workers' skills effectively, new ways had to be found to stimulate motivation. Companies were asking more from their employees; now they needed something that would compensate them for that extra effort, without increasing the price of the product. For many companies, sharing ownership met these objectives. It could provide workers with a powerful motivator and substantial financial benefit. And since it divided up firm equity, rather than adding to firm costs, it would not be reflected in the prices of products. In fact, studies of employee ownership were indicating that the concept could be very good for companies' bottom lines.

A 1978 study by Michael Conte and Arnold Tannenbaum of the University of Michigan's Survey Research Center, for instance, found that employee ownership companies were 1.5 times as profitable as conventional firms.[5] A study reported in the *Journal of Corporation Law* found that companies with ESOPs had twice the average annual productivity growth rate of comparable conventional firms.[6] A 1983 study by the National Center for Employee Ownership, (NCEO) reported that firms in which employees owned a majority of the stock generated three times more net new jobs per year than comparable conventional firms.[7] Another NCEO study, performed in 1984 for the New York Stock Exchange, found that publicly traded companies at least 10 percent employee owned outperformed 62 to 75 percent of their competitors, depending on the measure used.[8] A 1983 McKinsey and Company study found that one of the characteristics of America's fastest growing mid-sized companies was a relatively broad distribution of ownership.[9] A 1984 book entitled *The 100 Best Companies in America to Work For* identified employee ownership as one of the common characteristics of these firms.

These studies are only preliminary, of course, and one study still in progress has not found that employee ownership firms are more profitable, although it has found that they tend to stay in business longer.[10] Nonetheless, these investigations have been encouraging to people interested in experimenting with and evaluating employee ownership.

While the congressional intent of broadening the ownership of wealth and the corporate desire for new ways to organize work in an increasingly competitive world economy were the major forces behind the growth of employee ownership, two other factors were important as well. Starting slowly in the early 1970s and accelerating by the early 1980s, employees began buying plants that would otherwise close. Only about 1 percent of all employee ownership plans came about in this way, but these employee buyouts were dramatic events that focused press attention on the idea of employee ownership. At the same time that these buyouts were gaining strength, a new generation was graduating from college. A small but significant number of these graduates were not satisfied with traditional ways of doing business and turned to worker cooperatives as alternatives. Although most of these cooperatives remained small and concentrated more on making a statement than on making money, some did become successful enough to present an attractive alternative to conventional ownership and control patterns.

Employee Ownership Today

Employee ownership is, as noted, not what most people think. Far from being limited to dying companies or worker cooperatives, it is, in fact, a rapidly growing phenomenon in mainstream American business. We estimate that by the time this book reaches publication there will be 8,000 ESOPs covering 11 million workers. About 10 to 15 percent of these ESOPs will have a majority of their stock owned by employees.[11] The typical plan owns 15 to 40 percent of the stock. If we look at the percentage of employees, the numbers would change. Many employees participate in a special kind of ESOP known as a PAYSOP, which gives companies tax credits for contributions to provide employees with shares. These credits are limited to 0.5 percent of payroll, so most employees receive only a limited amount of stock. Since PAYSOPs tend to be established by very large employers, a majority of participants in ESOPs are actually only in PAYSOPs and own very little stock.[12] PAYSOPs are scheduled to expire in 1987.

Stock ownership in non-PAYSOP companies, however, is far from trivial. In 1985 NCEO completed a study of 145 representative ESOP firms and found that an employee making the 1983 median wage of $18,300 per year would accumulate $31,000 in stock after ten years in the typical ESOP.[13] The typical firm, we found, was contributing the equivalent of 10 percent of pay to the ESOP, and its stock value was growing at about 11 percent per year. We found little evidence to suggest that many firms were substituting their ESOPs for traditional pension plans, and almost all of the firms we have studied in depth have reported that their wages and benefits are competitive even without the ESOP.

As we shall see later, the financial return on an ESOP is the most important consideration to employees, but employee ownership can also be used to help create a more democratic firm. By law, employees must be able to vote their shares on all issues in public companies and on issues requiring more than a majority vote in private firms. About 15 percent of these private companies pass through full voting rights anyway, while some 50 percent of the majority employee-owned firms pass through full voting rights.[14]

We have less information about worker cooperatives and other kinds of employee ownership plans. There have been estimates of anywhere from a few hundred to a few thousand worker coops, most of which are very small and often in "alternative" businesses such as bookstores and restaurants. Other companies, such as Radio Shack, Lincoln Electric, and People Express, have plans in which most or all employees buy substantial amounts of stock and own a significant share of the company. Unfortunately, we have no systematic information about these companies.

The Structure of Employee Ownership Plans

Imagine that one day you decide it is time to share ownership with employees. Just how do you do it? Should everyone get stock, or should there be a waiting period? What about part-time or temporary employees? Should you give stock to employees or make them buy it? Should employees have to wait some period of time before the stock credited to them is actually theirs (this might help encourage people to stay with the company and, in effect, earn their stock)? How much should each person get—the same, as much as they earn, some combination? And what about voting? Should employees be able to vote the stock you give them, and if so, should people have one vote per share or one vote per person?

These are just the simplest of issues. The rules governing employee ownership are necessarily complex. But to understand how employee ownership is working it is necessary first to understand how employee ownership plans work. Since most plans are ESOPs, we will focus primarily on them.

ESOPs are found only in corporations, that is, not in partnerships or proprietorships. This is because only corporations have stock. Stock is a paper representation of the value of the company. In publicly held firms—those listed on a stock exchange—anyone can buy the company's stock. In closely held companies, stock ownership is restricted. The only people who can buy stock are the people the current owners agree to let buy it. Most companies are closely held.

For simplicity, assume you are the sole owner of a closely held company, Peter's Prodigious Pie Company. You've decided your employees should receive some equity in the business in return for the fruits of their labor. You've heard about ESOPs and they look good. The first thing you do is set up a trust fund. This will function something like a bank. You will make regular contributions of stock or cash to buy stock to this trust fund. If you contribute stock, you will normally just print additional shares, diluting your ownership in order to share ownership with employees.

The government will help you with this, because these contributions are, within limits, tax deductible. As a profitable company, you currently (1986) pay tax on 46 percent of your taxable profits (revenues minus expenses plus deductions). So every dollar's worth of stock that goes into the trust is a dollar on which you don't pay forty-six cents tax. You can make these contributions annually for up to 15 percent or 25 percent of the total payroll of the plan participants, or more if the plan is borrowing money. Moreover, by keeping the stock in the trust for an employee as long as he or she is employed, the employee does not have to pay any tax on it. In other words, if you share part of the pie, the government will put some of it back.

But the government wants something in return: It wants to make sure that employees are treated fairly. Remember all those questions posed at the outset of this section? The government has rules for all of these and more. First, you must allocate stock to all full-time employees over twenty-one who have worked at least one year. There are, however, some exceptions to this. For example you can exclude union members, provided they have a right to bargain in. As with other ESOP provisions, you can be more, but not less, generous in setting rules for your own company's ESOP. Second, you must allocate the shares according to relative pay (if you make $20,000 and I make $10,000, you get twice as much stock) or some more equal formula. Third, you must provide that the stock "vests" with employees over, generally, not less than ten years. Vesting is the process by which your employees acquire a gradually increasing right to their shares. In most plans vesting starts at 10 to 40 percent after one to four years and increases to 100 percent after ten years.

The stock is subject to the voting rights rules mentioned earlier. When employees leave the company they must recieve their stock or, in some cases, its cash value. If they get stock you must agree to buy it back from them at its fair market value, usually as determined by an outside appraisal. If the employee wants, he or she can offer it to someone else, but you can offer to match the price and have the first right to buy it.

There are many other rules as well, but most follow the basic tenet of ESOP law that the plans be for the benefit of employees. Most people find them complex but not unreasonable. They sound even more reasonable in light of all the things you can do with an ESOP.

Uses of an ESOP

Perhaps you have simply come to the conclusion that employee benefits must be raised, but you lack the cash to do it. Your company is expanding and you want to put the cash into growth. So why not share the growth?

With an ESOP you can simply issue additional shares of stock. If there are 10,000 shares of Peter's Prodigious, for instance, you might ask your board of directors to authorize an additional 2,500. You could then issue 500 shares a year to the

ESOP, deducting their values from your taxable income. If the shares are worth $100 each, you can deduct $50,000 for five years. If you have fifty employees participating in the ESOP, they would receive, on average, $1,000 each in their accounts each year. At the end of five years, you and the board could decide if you wanted to issue additional shares.

In this example your company would save $23,000 in federal taxes, plus state taxes where applicable. You would now own 80 percent of the stock—10,000 out of 12,500 shares. Your employees would own part of the company, and hopefully, the motivation that provides will help the company grow so that your initial contribution will actually enable you to own a smaller piece of a bigger pie-making company. It is important to remember, though, that when employees leave the company, the company or the ESOP must repurchase their shares. While these repurchases can be tax deductible as well, they can still represent a substantial cost to the company. Because of this, ESOPs normally work best in companies that are growing. Of the cases discussed in later chapters, Quad/Graphics, Lowe's, the Evaluation Research Corporation, and Up-Right have used ESOPs as additional benefit plans.

But let's say that you face a different problem, namely, retirement. After building your company from scratch, you would now like gradually to withdraw from it. For years you have been putting everything into the business, so now you have machines, a building, employees, a good name, and so on. But how do you turn those things into cash for retirement? You have to sell your stock. There are several ways to do this: You could find another company to buy you out, which is not always easy, even for profitable firms. Even if a buyer can be found, you may not want to see your company and your employees taken over, especially by someone who might lay off some of your people, change your company's name, or otherwise remake what you worked so hard to create. The buyer also might want you to leave right after the sale, not allowing you to gradually wind down your involvement. You could have the company buy your shares, but the company would have to do it with more expensive after-tax dollars and you might have to pay ordinary income tax on the sale, rather than capital gains tax, which is 60 percent less. You could pass it on to an heir, who would eventually buy you out, but most people don't have one interested in taking over the business. Finally, you could just liquidate—sell the machines, the building, the recipes, the product name, and so on. But even if that works out acceptably financially, it is hardly an attractive option.

An ESOP is a good alternative. You would have the company make tax deductible cash contributions to the trust, or have the trust borrow money, as explained below. The trust would then buy your shares, either all at once (if it borrowed the money) or gradually (if you contributed cash). If you reinvest the proceeds of the sale in the stock of other companies, you can defer any tax until the new stock is sold, and then you pay only capital gains tax—a maximum of 20 percent in 1986. If you don't reinvest, then you pay capital gains right away, but that is better than paying ordinary income tax (a maximum of 50 percent), as you would if the company bought your stock without the ESOP. In short, the company saves money in buying you out, you save money in taxes, the employees get the company, and you can withdraw from the business as gradually or quickly as you like. Given all these advantages, it is not surprising that this is the most common use for an ESOP. Allied Plywood, M. W. Carr, and Fastener Industries all originated this way.

ESOPs can also borrow money. Assume that you decide you need some new pie-making machinery. Normally, you would go to your banker and have the company take out a loan. When it repaid the loan, it could deduct the interest portion. Then you might set up a bonus plan so employees could have a piece of the pie. With an ESOP the company would have the ESOP trust borrow the money, which it would use to buy newly issued shares of stock in Peter's Prodigious. Peter's would use the money from the sale to buy the machinery. The company would guarantee the lender that it would make contributions to the trust sufficient to enable it to repay the loan. These contributions, within limits, are tax deductible so, in effect, you can deduct both interest and principal on the loan. On a $1 million loan, you would save $460,000 in taxes. Your banker will be pleased, too, because banks and other commercial lenders can deduct 50 percent of the interest income they receive from loans to ESOPs. At least some banks are passing on some of this deduction to borrowers, resulting in loan rates 10 to 20 percent below what they would be without the ESOP. At the same time, your employees would become owners, getting not just a piece of the pie but a part of the pie-making machinery.

Of course, you will have to repurchase the shares in the ESOP one day (unless you become a public company so that employees can sell their shares on the market), and the issuance of the new shares will cause a dilution in your holdings. If the new machinery helps you grow, the ESOP benefits should more than outweigh these concerns; if you do not grow, however, the ESOP could present a greater liability than conventional debt financing would.

A similar approach could be used if Peter's were a profitable division of another company that the parent wanted to sell. Here, Peter's employees would set up a shell company, which would in turn set up an ESOP to borrow enough money to buy the assets of Peter's Prodigious from its parent. The ESOP would then exchange these assets for all the newly issued stock in the shell company. This approach is appealing to the parent because it can be paid a fair market price by the ESOP. If Peter's were put on the market and did not sell quickly, key management people might leave and employee morale might sink, causing a decline in the value of the company to another buyer. Managers and employees at other divisions might begin to wonder if they were next and start looking for other employment. With an ESOP sale, though, they might even look forward to a divestiture.

These four uses—providing an additional employee benefit, buying out a retiring owner, borrowing money to raise capital, and divesting a subsidiary—account for virtually all ESOPs, but most of the press attention has focused on more dramatic events. Imagine, for instance, that Peter's comes upon hard times. Perhaps management has failed to react to the latest culinary fad or has sold Peter's to a big conglomerate that now finds bioengineering more interesting than pie making. Faced with imminent closing, Peter's employees decide to make an offer to buy their company. We estimate that there have been about seventy employee buyouts of troubled firms in the last decade, of which 80 percent are still in business; about half of those that are not were sold as ongoing companies to other owners.

There are a number of reasons why employees might be able to make a go of a firm that previous management could not: New management could be brought in; the burden of conglomerate overhead or lack of interest could be removed; employee motivation and involvement might increase productivity or generate new ideas; employees might be willing to make concessions to themselves that they would be unwilling to make to other owners. But Peter's employees are not likely to be able to come up with the cash to buy the company, so how will they ever have a chance to try any of these options? An ESOP, again, provides the answer. As in the divestiture case above, the employees set up a new shell company, which sets up an ESOP. The ESOP borrows the money needed to buy the plant and exchanges the assets for stock in the new company. The new company then makes contributions to the ESOP so that it can repay the loan. Employees do not put up any of their own money directly, although they may take wage or benefit concessions to help enable the company to repay the loan. Of course, this is not quite as simple as it sounds. The employees will have to pay for a feasibility study to see whether the buyout is practical and persuade lenders to loan money. In some cases, the employees may need to find some equity investors as well. Several states now have programs to help with this, and there is limited federal money as well. Most employee buyout efforts, however, never get past the talking stage.

Less dramatically, employees can take wage concessions in return for stock at an ongoing company to help keep it going. This has become very common in the airline, trucking, and steel industries, where it has resulted in some employees' receiving major ownership interests and seats on the boards of many of these industries' largest firms. The argument here, of course, is that if employees agree to take concessions, they are, in effect, making an investment in the firm and should get stock in consideration for this investment.

The last, and least common, use of an ESOP goes well beyond most of the Peter's Prodigiouses of this world. In recent years the leveraged buyout has become the most glamorous of financing techniques. Usually, management of a large, public company will arrange for a loan to buy out all the stock of the company, using the company itself as collateral. Sometimes this is done to prevent a hostile takeover; sometimes simply because management wants a chance to own the company. In some cases, an ESOP has been used to buy part or all of the stock, resulting in several major companies' becoming significantly employee owned. For instance, Dan River is 70 percent employee owned, Parsons Engineering 100 percent, Blue Bell 30 percent, and U.S. Sugar 43 percent.

The attraction of the ESOP is obvious. An LBO creates a company with an enormous debt burden. An ESOP can help the company get a cheaper loan (because of the deduction for banks) and then repay it in pretax dollars. Sometimes companies whose pension plans have "excess funding" terminate the plans, using some of the funds to buy annuities for the employees equal to their interest in the plans and the excess to buy stock through the ESOP. In some cases new pension plans are set up; in others the ESOP becomes the only pension. In almost every instance, Parsons being the most notable exception, employees do not have the right to vote their shares. In many cases, management is also able to buy class B stock at a much lower price than the ESOP. The B stock, which is not part of the ESOP, has different risks and requires an up-front investment, but many believe the price differentials typical of these deals cannot be justified.

The use of an ESOP in these cases has become very controversial. Critics contend that these plans are really designed primarily to entrench management rather than benefit employees. Defenders argue that these LBOs would be done anyway, and pensions would still be terminated. With an ESOP, at least the employees get something. The controversy has led to a Labor Department promise for new rules for these kinds of plans.

ESOPs and Their Critics

While the LBOs have raised the most eyebrows, ESOPs in general have become more controversial in recent years. Critics often argue that ESOPs do not provide a sufficiently secure retirement plan, that employees do not have enough control over their shares in most plans, and that many plans are structured so that management reaps more than its fair share of the benefits. There are too little data to determine whether ESOPs are commonly substituted for other kinds of benefit plans. Our impression is that few companies that would have had a defined benefit pension plan set up an ESOP instead, but many companies have an ESOP instead of profit sharing. Which kind of plan is better is both a philosophical and an empirical question. Data noted earlier, however, indicate that ESOP participants do quite well relative to recipients of other kinds of employee benefit plans, including profit sharing. These data are limited to the last twelve years, of course, and only some ESOP participants have actually cashed out their shares. The numbers, though, do seem encouraging.

Other criticisms are more subjective, based on individual views of what an ESOP should be. Is it intended as a means of democratizing the workplace or spreading ownership? Is it proper to allow substantial benefits to managers and current owners in order to encourage them to share at least some ownership with workers, or should rules require a much more equal sharing? Clearly, the more restrictive the rules and the fewer benefits to managers, the fewer companies will set up ESOPs and the fewer employees will become owners. This ownership stake can be very substantial, and it is the financial aspect of ownership that matters most to employees. Moreover, while most ESOPs are not very democratic, many are, and many more workers are in democratic or partly democratic ESOPs than any other kind of democratic corporate arrangement.

Any tax-based program will face the problem of companies using it for limited ends that fall far short of the ideals behind the incentives or the ideals some people may think the incentives should be based on. The question must be whether the cost of these incentives, including the abuses of them, justifies the benefits. We think that ESOPs have more than justified themselves in these terms, mostly by accomplishing a significant distribution of ownership to people who would never otherwise be owners, but also by, in a number of cases, helping create new models of what a truly efficient and equitable company can be. Many of these models are discussed in this book.

Worker Cooperatives

While the principal motivating force behind ESOPs has been the desire to share the ownership of wealth, the principal force behind worker cooperatives has been the desire to share power. In France, Italy, and the Mondragon region of Spain there are extensive and very successful worker cooperative sectors. Worker cooperatives in the United States have been around since the nineteenth century. For the most part, they have been limited to very small businesses. In the 1970s many were established in alternative businesses by people seeking to market products they considered more socially responsible. Most of these coops have short life expectancies, either because they have difficulty competing or because the low pay and long hours they often demand make it difficult to retain employees over several years.

Recently, however, worker cooperatives have been set up in more conventional businesses, sometimes in conjunction wtih an ESOP financial structure. Some of the cooperatives have been startups; others have been responses to plant closings. Although the number of these cooperatives is small, they have been more successful than the alternative business coops and have demonstrated that this business form can compete.

In worker cooperatives only workers can be owners, although there can be nonowning workers, often seasonal or part-time employees. Each worker-owner has one and only one vote. A portion of net earnings is returned annually to the owners, either directly or by being placed into an account. The coop pays no tax on these earnings. Funds in the account are paid interest, usually at below market rates. If there are losses they are subtracted from the accounts. When a worker leaves he or she gets whatever is in the account. In many cooperatives workers must purchase a share of stock from a departing owner or the company, often out of wage deferrals. In successful companies these shares can become very expensive, sometimes making it difficult to attract new owners.

A different approach has the new workers become members of the cooperative, paying an affordable fee into an account. No one is considered an "owner" in the conventional sense. These coops almost always use the accounts system described above for handling retained earnings, although they usually pay a portion of net earnings directly to the employee; since these earnings are taxable, even if paid into the accounts, receiving some in cash helps pay the taxes.

All coops have a one-owner or one-member/one-vote structure, but there are differences in how this setup translates into corporate governance. In smaller coops workers generally comprise the board and make most decisions collectively, often by consensus. In larger coops there are sometimes outside board members, elected by the workers, and more delegation of power to individuals and committees. Sometimes a nonowning general manager is appointed by the board. A common pattern is to start by trying to involve everyone in decisions and then move gradually toward a system in which responsibility and authority are assigned, subject to review by the board or the workers.

The best-known cooperatives in the United States are the Northwest Plywood Coops.[15] Established mostly in the 1940s, there have been as many as thirty plywood coops, each employing up to several hundred workers. They each had workers buy their shares, appointed a nonowning general manager, and paid all owners equally, although many hired a substantial number of nonowning workers. Work by Katrina Berman indicates that these coops were 30 percent more productive than their conventionally owned competitors.

Today only a dozen of the plywood coops remain. Some

were victims of their own prosperity: their shares became so expensive that no buyers could be found for the shares of departing owners. Selling out to another company was sometimes the only solution. Others found ways around sellouts, usually by allowing employees to borrow from the company the money to buy the shares of departing owners and repay it out of wage deferrals. Some of these companies, however, fell victim to the severe depression in the housing industry in the late 1970s and early 1980s. Despite their problems, the plywood coops, on the whole, have been remarkably successful.

More recently, cooperatives have been used to buy failing firms. The O & O (Owned and Operated) supermarkets in Philadelphia originated this way. When A & P announced it would close its Philadelphia-area stores the local union suggested that it be allowed to buy at least some of them. Ultimately, the company agreed to reopen some of the stores under a new name and with a new, innovative labor agreement. Employees were able to purchase two of the stores and open them as worker cooperatives. Both did quite well and a third O & O store that was started from scratch opened in 1985.

The O & O stores require each worker to put up $5,000 to become a member and have used that fee plus conventional debt financing to raise capital. Worker buyouts at Seymour Specialty Wire in Connecticut and Atlas Chain in Pennsylvania used a different approach. Here the employees set up shell companies which in turn set up ESOPs to borrow the needed capital. While workers have ESOP accounts, the stock is voted by the ESOP trustee at the direction of the workers on a one-person, one-vote arrangement rather than the one-share, one-vote method used in most ESOPs. These two companies have thus combined the financial structure of an ESOP with the governance plan of a coop. This concept was pioneered by the Solar Center, one of the cases presented in this book. Given the weight of ESOP tax benefits, this approach seems likely to become common in those larger companies that want to operate as cooperatives. In smaller companies (under ten to fifteen employes), the coop structure will likely continue because its legal costs and complexity are much less than those of an ESOP.

Making Employee Ownership Work

There are several levels at which employee ownership can be said to "work." It can, for instance, simply accomplish financial planning/tax objectives. It can also help increase profitability, make work more satisfying, broaden the ownership of wealth, or provide the basis for democratic control of a firm. Which of these goals it accomplishes depends in part on what the company and its workers expect from employee ownership.

The financial planning/tax goals are essentially self-realizing. Achieving greater productivity or profitability, however, is more complicated. Research on these questions is now underway, both at the National Center for Employee Ownership and elsewhere. At this point a significant amount of ownership for employees, greater employee participation, and effective communications programs all seem potentially important, but definitive conclusions cannot yet be drawn.

At the employee level, however, there are more data. As part of a major project on employee ownership described below, NCEO evaluated the impact of ownership on employee attitudes, motivation, and behavior. Complete results are reported in *Employee Ownership in America: The Equity Solution.*[16] Several key factors emerged from this study.

First, for most employees the critical feature of an employee ownership plan is money. The primary factor accounting for differences in employee attitudes toward ownership is how much stock the employees receive each year. Control, participation, company size and culture, and other variables matter less. This suggests that employees do not usually want the responsibility of running their company any more than most citizens want the responsibility of running their government. Of course, that is not to say that employees do not value participation or want the right to have some check on management authority; it means that the most important consideration is the added wealth employee ownership can provide.

Conversely, some employees do place a high value on control. Many of them join cooperatives explicitly for that reason. In buyouts or concession arrangements employees want to be sure to protect their investment; they might be more than normally suspicious of management. Moreover, participation opportunities at the job level do seem important in most firms, though, as noted, not as important as financial rewards. Finally, allowing employees a say in management can have a positive affect on employee attitudes and, perhaps more important, open a valuable line of communication between workers and managers. Managers of these more democratic firms, in fact, unanimously agree that this input contributes to the companies' bottom line.

Company culture also seems to matter. In many of the cases discussed in this book managers believe employees *deserve* to be owners. They do not see ownership as a benevolent bestowal on the part of enlightened leaders, but rather as a logical component of good management. Management can convey the feeling that employees are seen more as equals and less as hired help in many ways. For example, the company president walks the floor sincerely seeking employee ideas; special management prerequisites such as closer parking and separate lunchrooms are abolished; and all employees are called "associates" or "managers."

Communication is also critical. Employee ownership plans can be complex. If employees do not understand their plan, they can hardly be motivated by it. The companies with the most effective plans tend, therefore, to be the ones with the most effective communications programs. These efforts must be two-way (employees must be able to give their views and have them heard) and must be repeated often.

In fact, overall, it is fair to say that the best plans are those that provide constant reinforcement of the ownership idea. Employees receive regular, substantial stock contributions; have participation opportunities on the job; are treated as owners by managers and supervisors; and are frequently and effectively reminded of their ownership stake in the firm. Ownership becomes a constantly renewed process rather than a discrete event that happens once a year when employees receive an account update.

Employee Ownership and Social Change

If employee ownership does work as suggested here, it can have a dramatic impact on society. As noted, employees can build substantial capital estates, companies can be more productive, and, at least in some cases, firms can be democratized.

But these social changes have been accomplished within a distinctly conventional framework. Employee ownership has been endorsed by everyone from Ronald Reagan to Ted Kennedy, from the New York Stock Exchange to the Teamsters Union, from Paul Volcker to Pope John Paul II. It has attained this broad support by tying economic self-interest to a social goal. Rather than stressing altruistic, ideological notions, most employee ownership advocates focus on how it can make everyone—workers, companies, existing shareholders—better off. For this reason, the idea is not very threatening to most groups except, to some extent, to organized labor, whose attitude is more ambivalent than hostile. Some unions fear that ownership can coopt workers, but others have embraced the idea as a new bargaining tool.

Even on the broader issue of employee control, ownership has made significant inroads. If only some 400 companies are owned *and* controlled by their employees, at least that is 400 more than are controlled by workers but not owned by them. Moreover, a growing number of major firms in which employees have less than majority ownership are allowing employee representation on their boards of directors—a situation found in only a handful of conventional firms. It is fair to say that in this country employee ownership has been the only legitimate method for democratizing the firm at the management level. It has accomplished this goal not just in cooperatives but in hundreds of otherwise mainline and often quite large companies. It can do this, it seems, because employees as owners are perceived to be much less threatening than employees as nonowning workers. In a number of cases, this process has been gradual, with companies first sharing ownership and later sharing control as well. The second step is made much easier by the first.

This gradual model of social change is perhaps too slow for some and too meandering for others. Yet it has accomplished more than almost anyone anticipated ten years ago and a great deal more than the usually quixotic "holistic" approaches to social concerns advocated by some, approaches that require wholesale social and economic change. These may be intellectually appealing, but they are not very practical. While employee ownership is still only a minor part of the economy, it has gained a clear and legitimate foothold as a practical, businesslike approach. If it demonstrates that it can live up to expectations, it could well become a common means of doing business.

Methods

The cases that follow will not only help assess whether employee ownership is living up to these expectations but will also provide some guidelines and examples to help assure that it does. The companies selected for these cases have diverse goals for their plans. Our goal is to assess how and if they achieved their goals. We also examine ownership from an employee's point of view. Is ownership a meaningful incentive for the employees? Does it make work more satisfying?

Most of the studies draw on a larger project of the National Center for Employee Ownership, whose staff and research associates conducted over fifty case studies. The project was funded by the National Institute for Mental Health. The purpose of the study was to determine what factors make some employee ownership plans more effective than others. Effectiveness was primarily measured by the impact of the plan on employee attitudes and behaviors, as measured by a 140-item survey administered to all or most of a company's employees, except in very large firms, where a random sample was taken. As reported in many of the cases that follow, we measured such factors as employee attitudes toward their firm and their job, work motivation, turnover intention, and perceptions of levels of employee participation. We also interviewed the firms' CEOs for information on how the plans and the companies operate.

This book includes some of the companies that were studied in the NCEO research project as well as a few that have not been analyzed so intensively. The cases were not selected as representatives of the employee ownership phenomenon but as indicators of the range of possibilities for employee ownership. Most published work on employee ownership has focused narrowly on employee buyouts of failing firms. This book provides an overview of the wider use of the concept. We hope most of all that these cases will convey both the excitement and the potential problems employee ownership can generate. Employee ownership is an emerging phenomenon, its growth and direction far from certain. This book begins to chart just how this innovative concept will develop.

2

THE M. W. CARR COMPANY: EVOLVING WORKER AWARENESS

"We are now in process of trying to educate 220 workers. Ownership means more than sharing in the profits of the company. There must be an attitudinal change on the part of everyone who works here."[1] This quote from a manager at the M. W. Carr Company, a 100 percent employee-owned manufacturer of picture frames in Somerville, Massachusetts, typifies the attitudes the company's leadership has had for decades. Management has been introducing various forms of employee participation and employee ownership into the company for thirty-five years. So when the workers became 100 percent owners in 1981 it was not an abrupt change in company organization, but one more step in a continuing process of innovation.

The M. W. Carr Company manufactures 15,000 wood and metal picture frames a day. The company generates over $15 million in annual sales and has captured about 20 percent of the high-quality picture frame market. Martin Wales Carr started the business in 1869, and three generations of the Carr family managed it before Louis B. Carr became president in 1946. During World War II a shortage of raw materials had nearly devastated the family business; in fact, it was technically insolvent when Louis Carr took over.

In an effort to save the failing company, Carr slashed his salary and looked for new ways to attract and keep good labor.

This chapter draws heavily on several previous studies of the M. W. Carr Company: Megan Campbell, Sergio Storch, and a story in the *Boston Globe*.

"We couldn't afford to pay much, so we had to get the people involved." In 1948 Carr began two experiments that shaped the character of labor relations at M. W. Carr for decades. The first experiment was a group incentive system, which Carr later changed to an individual incentive system. Carr set a norm for the average worker's productivity. Then, as an incentive, he evenly split between the workers and the company the value of any production above 80 percent of the norm. Today many workers augment their wages by as much as 30 percent from incentive bonuses. And the company doesn't ratchet up the norm to keep bonus payments down. In fact, the Carr Company adjusts the standards only when new techniques drastically change productivity.

The Carr/Craft dinners were Louis Carr's second experiment that first year. At these monthly get-togethers, named for the firm's craftsmen, Carr met with workers chosen to represent each area of the shop. Carr recognized from the start the importance of communication between employees and managers. He encouraged workers to take part in the dinners, and before they were discontinued twenty-five years later, between two-thirds and three-fourths of the employees had participated. These dinners were the seed of the May employee profit-sharing banquet, which, since 1981, have doubled as the annual Carr Company stockholders' meetings.

With Carr's two experiments and a lot of hard work, the company made a profit in 1949 and continued to improve its financial position during the early 1950s. As the company grew more stable, Carr wanted to give its employees some security but could not afford the fixed payments of a regular pension plan. So in 1954 the M. W. Carr Company established a profit-sharing plan for its fifty employees. Under the plan the company retained the first 6 percent on its equity out of any profits earned. Of the remaining profits, the company contributed 40 percent to the profit-sharing plan and the plan allocated profits to individual employee accounts according to a formula based on salary and years of service. At first the company made only cash contributions to the profit-sharing plan. But Carr wanted employees to own stock in the company and began making contributions half in cash and half in stock.

The productivity incentives, the dinners, and the profit-sharing plan initiated a tradition of looking out for employees at M. W. Carr. Over the years the company offered a number of other perks as well. Employees can set their own hours and choose their holidays. Many supervisory and managerial positions are filled in-house, and now over half the managers are people who started in hourly positions. Also, there have been no layoffs, even during slack periods, so employees feel that they can count on their jobs.

Despite all these innovations, Carr was dissatisfied with the firm's employee benefit plans. He remembers that in the early 1970s, "We began to realize that one thing was still missing. The money was there, but it was still 'your' [Carr's] company. We decided to explore the whole concept of employee ownership." Carr began reading books and attending meetings about the newly passed legislation creating Employee Stock Ownership Plans, and he concluded an ESOP would be right for the company.

Deciding on an ESOP was only the first step, according to Carr. "The next thing was to work with our own management and familiarize them with the concept. That took a lot of time and effort. You have to really believe in the concept, otherwise you shouldn't get involved." What is Carr's concept of an ESOP? He believes that "a lot of these [ESOPs] went in for the wrong reasons, such as tax avoidance." But, he says, "Ours is the real McCoy. My contention is that the greatest problem in the capitalist system is that there are too few capitalists." So in an effort to "create 200 new capitalists," M. W. Carr launched its ESOP in 1977.

During the late 1970s Louis Carr began to prepare for his retirement, but none of his children wanted to take his place in the business. Several acquirers approached Carr, but he "decided not to go that route because we had good people who had been here a long time." Like many retiring owners in his position, Carr wanted his company to remain independent. Moreover, he believed that the employees "have helped make this company what it is, and that they should have a chance to benefit from any future efforts to keep it going." So when Carr retired in 1981 he sold his remaining shares to the company. The employees, with their holdings in the profit-sharing plan and the ESOP, became 100 percent owners of M. W. Carr.

The Ownership Structure

The profit-sharing plan and the ESOP have identical allocation and vesting structures. Employees are eligible to participate in the plans during their first year of work, and they become vested in their accounts relatively quickly. Workers have 20 percent vesting after two years and 20 percent each year thereafter, with full vesting after six years of employment. The plans allocate shares and profits to employees' accounts according to a point system based on salary and tenure: three points for each year worked and one point for each $100 in annual salary. This allocation method rewards pay differentials without handing managers a controlling interest in the company. Indeed, production workers now own 51 percent of M. W. Carr and foremen another 21 percent, with middle- and upper-level managers owning the remaining 22 percent.

Today the M. W. Carr Company ploughs back 20 percent of its annual pretax profits into the profit-sharing trust. This trust has diversified holdings, including the Carr Company shares it acquired before the ESOP. Over a period of six years the company is also contributing the remaining Carr family shares to the ESOP trust at a rate of over $250,000 worth per year. The company holds these shares as treasury stock—that is, as shares owned by the corporation—until it transfers them to the ESOP. In 1983 the profit-sharing plan and the ESOP were worth about $5.5 million.

The M. W. Carr Company guarantees employees the right to participate democratically in company policymaking. Though not a legal requirement since the company is closely held, employees at Carr instruct the ESOP trustees how to vote their shares on a one-share, one-vote basis. Beginning in 1982 the employees elected the board of directors. Workers also participate in labor/management committees for health and safety issues, social events, and the company newsletter.

When workers retire or leave the company they may do one of three things with their vested accounts. Within six months employees may sell their shares back to the ESOP at the most recent fair market-appraised value. Alternatively, they may hold their stock and sell it back within three months after the next appraisal. If former employees choose to hold their stock beyond this time, the ESOP is no longer legally obliged to repurchase it. However, individuals may then negotiate to sell their shares to outsiders, although the ESOP retains the right of first refusal.

Employee Attitudes

M. W. Carr's managers are generally enthusiastic about employee ownership and optimistic about its potential. They have relatively more shares, are more experienced with stock ownership, and seem to be more willing to defer rewards. Still, some managers were initially uneasy with the idea of employee ownership and the workers' control that came with it. To ameliorate their discomfort, Louis Carr began training his managers for employee ownership long before initiating the ESOP. One manager recalls:

> *When I came here I felt that the company was being run with a very weak hand, that the workers were kind of directing things, that they were taking liberties that I felt were unfair. I came from a very hard working blue collar culture, I put myself through college and worked very hard. We never had much money and we worked hard for the money we earned. When I came here I saw people abusing their jobs. They weren't working as hard as I thought they should work, they were taking liberties which I thought they shouldn't do. That bothered me. And slowly the person whom I was reporting to began to cajole*

and twist and redirect my thinking. That philosophy took several years to trickle down to me. Now I feel very strong about it.

I felt that because of the position I had in the company, I should have many, many more benefits than the other workers. But they kept on saying, "No, whatever benefits you have the next person should have." And I said, "No. I worked for it, I went to school," and so on. I don't feel that way now. I can't say that I am 100 percent in favor of everything being equal, but I think that everyone should be rewarded by the pay, and if there are any other benefits like profit, it should be distributed across the board to everybody.

Management at Carr sees communications with the rank and file as its main task for the next few years. While managers believe that employee ownership has increased employee motivation, they don't think it has reached its full potential. Managers want employees to realize that they own this business. As Carr put it in 1981, "We're trying to pass decisionmaking down the line as far as we can. Each person becomes a quality control station." In 1983 the company scheduled six employee ownership awareness meetings, which were attended by one top manager, two middle managers, and fifteen nonmanagerial employees. The company also publishes a newsletter and distributes financial information to employees.

In 1981 and 1983 the National Center for Employee Ownership (NCEO) surveyed employees at M. W. Carr to gauge their attitudes about their jobs and their employee ownership plans. The two sets of survey results suggest that the company's efforts at communicating the employee ownership concept have begun to pay off. In 1981 respondents had a high level of job satisfaction but showed little interest in ownership, per se. More than 90 percent of the employees responding said that if they were job hunting they would choose to work at Carr. But more than half the respondents felt like an employee rather than an owner, and less than one-fifth cited the ESOP as being important.

At the time the employees were new to being 100 percent owners; Louis Carr had just retired and sold his holdings to the company. Many employees thought of the ESOP as part of the benefits package, not as ownership, and they had trouble distinguishing the ESOP from the profit-sharing plan. Some said: "They are both ways to share the company profits. One way you get cash, one way you get stock." For some, the profit-sharing plan was more important than the ESOP: "Since in the end it all comes down to money, I'd rather have a large amount in my profit-sharing account and forget about this stock business."

Before 1981 Carr employees had no formal decisionmaking authority, and at the time of the survey that year the company was preparing to hold its first employee vote for the board of directors. During interviews workers did not attribute much significance to the upcoming vote. One comment on the voting seems to capture many workers' feelings about worker participation and worker ownership in general at the time: "Management thinks this is a big deal, like a symbol or something. But I won't really know what I'm voting for. Stocks, finance, business decisions: what are they all about? Do I want to learn? Well, maybe. I haven't thought that much about it."

Over the next two years employees had time to think about it as they gained experience with employee ownership: they attended ownership awareness meetings, elected the board of directors, read newsletters, and participated in annual shareholders' meetings. When NCEO returned with its new questionnaire in 1983, employees evinced more interest in their role as owners. The differences in employee responses may or may not be statistically significant (NCEO has not yet done that analysis), but they do suggest that the continual efforts of Carr's management are making a change.

In responding to the new survey, employees, on average, neither agreed nor disagreed with the statement, "I feel like a real owner in this company." While this is hardly a ringing endorsement of the ESOP, it is a marked improvement over the 1981 attitude, when four-fifths of the respondents said they felt like employees. Moreover, in 1983 most employees said that they were proud to own stock in Carr, that owning stock made their work more satisfying and made them more interested in the company's financial performance.

On questions of worker participation, survey responses suggest that workers' desire for influence has evolved as workers have become more sophisticated in their role as employee owners. The pattern of responses shows that employees are relatively more satisfied with their decisionmaking role in areas where they have been participating for years. For example, workers and managers have been working together on social events since the time of the Carr/Craft dinners, and workers' responses show that their desired level of influence over social events is only slightly higher than the level they already have. But workers would like somewhat more influence over working conditions and the way they perform their own jobs, preferring to decide these matters with managers rather than simply being asked their opinions. Also, workers believe that when it comes to pay, the selection of supervisors, and setting long-term policy, they have no say and only receive information about management's decisions after the fact. In these areas, too, workers would like to have more influence, at least to express their opinions.

Conclusion

Ever since Louis Carr's two experiments in 1948, the M. W. Carr Company has been developing creative programs of participation and ownership. Each feature grew naturally from its predecessors—from incentive programs and Carr/Craft dinners, to profit sharing and the ESOP and management training, to 100 percent employee ownership and employee-owner awareness meetings.

Because the company is still experimenting and learning, the full impact of 100 percent employee ownership at Carr may not be felt for years. The ultimate efficacy of employee ownership in terms of productivity, increased participation, worker attitudes, and feelings of entitlement cannot yet be measured. Carr instituted the ESOP from the top down in a friendly environment. Still, many employees are reserving judgment about where it will lead. As one worker cautiously observed in 1981:

> *I'm sure the ESOP is a good thing. But I'm not sure what being an owner means. I didn't start this business, although I've worked here for many years. So, now I'm an owner. But, I don't feel any different. Do my supervisors think I'm different? Basically, the ESOP increases my assets. And being an owner makes me feel more connected; I have more stake in the company. But participation? Ownership? Ask me again in five years.*

3

EVALUATION RESEARCH CORPORATION: EMPLOYEE OWNERSHIP AS A BENEFIT PLAN

Evaluation Research Corporation (ERC) is a professional services company headquartered in Vienna, Virginia, with offices across the United States and in Australia. Created in 1976, ERC now employs over 600 people and in 1983 had revenues exceeding $28 million. ERC provides professional and technical services in engineering, logistics, information sciences, computer-aided engineering, and energy and environmental science. Its professional staff of engineers, logisticians, energy specialists, analysts, computer programmers, software designers, physicists, and economists work under contract for the military, nondefense government agencies, and the private sector. Since 1985 ERC has marketed products as well as services, including an electronic technical publishing system based on the Apollo Domain computer that automates the integration of text and graphics.

ERC's founder and president, Jack Aalseth, knew from the beginning that people would be the firms's basic resource. "I wanted to attract good people to the company and didn't have a big name. So I had to give something up—equity."[1] Aalseth, who once owned 100 percent of the company's stock, now owns less than 10 percent. Employees, individually and through an employee stock ownership plan (ESOP), own about one-third of the stock; the rest is widely distributed after a successful public offering in 1982. Aalseth has no regrets about sharing ownership. "You don't grow companies this fast with this quality without offering more than a paycheck," he points out. It makes a lot more sense, he argues, to own a small piece of a large pie than all of a small one. The company's growth in employment reflects its growth in earnings and net shareholders' equity. Net earnings increased from $69,000 in 1977 to $361,000 in 1981; total shareholders' equity grew from $184,000 to $1.92 million during those same years, and earnings per share almost tripled.

Many factors account for this success, and Aalseth believes that employee ownership was significant among them. Employees own stock at ERC in various ways, including through direct purchases and stock options, but the ESOP is the mechanism used to distribute ownership broadly among employees.

ERC's ESOP owned 19 percent of the company's stock in 1981. Aalseth says that "a large part of ERC's growth is attributable to ESOP capital and to ownership's impact on employee productivity." The ESOP was established in 1978, largely to attract qualified people. At that time other firms could offer better salaries, security, and fringe benefits, so ERC compensated with ownership. All ERC employees over twenty years old and with 1,000 hours of service are eligible to participate in the ESOP. Shares are allocated according to relative compensation. Vesting is fast, ESOP participants being 20 percent vested after their second year and 100 percent vested after their sixth.

In 1982 ERC contributed 6 percent of annual covered payroll to ESOP participants. Normally the company hopes to contribute 8 percent of covered payroll, but contributions cannot exceed the firm's aggregate after-tax profits. Aalseth sees this system as a good way to make clear the link between company performance and employee rewards. Advertisements proclaiming in bold letters "EMPLOYEE OWNED/EMPLOYEE ORIENTED/ THE TEAM THAT COUNTS ON YOU" reflect ERC's belief in the ESOP's value as a recruiting tool. "Our employee benefit package," the ad continues, "features a company funded employee stock ownership plan (ESOP) which increases in value each year as we grow."

Making Employees Aware of the ESOP

ERC's emphasis on the ESOP makes it critical that employees understand just what they are getting. One of the most vexing problems employee ownership companies face is that many employees have little experience with stock ownership and corporate finance. The complexity of rules governing ESOPs compounds the problem. Employees are often skeptical of what appears to be getting something for nothing. Clearly, even the best-structured, most generous ESOP will fail to motivate an employee unless it is well communicated and understood.

Aalseth notes that even at ERC, with a relatively highly educated workforce, the ESOP "needs a better marketing job. . . . They need a constant flow of information about the ESOP to understand it." As required by law, the company gives each employee a summary plan description explaining how the plan works. Employees may also inspect the plan itself, and the company newsletter features a regular ESOP column reporting such things as the amount of the annual contribution and answering common questions. Most important, the company sponsors regular question and answer sessions during working hours so employees can directly question ESOP trust officers about the plan.

In addition, two of the five members of the trust committee overseeing plan administration are ERC employees; the other three come from ERC's board of directors. ERC shares financial information with employees, providing quarterly statements, annual reports, and periodic summaries in the newsletter.

Other companies have used guest speakers, developed slide presentations or films, held annual ESOP meetings, or developed special booklets on the ESOP. Few ESOP companies are completely satisfied with their efforts; some hardly make an effort at all. Effective communication is the first step any company must take to make an ESOP work.

Voting Rights

Giving employees voting rights is an excellent way to increase awareness of their ownership position. Being able to attend shareholder meetings and receiving proxy material reminds employees (even if they do not attend or vote) that they are owners. Where employees own a minority of shares, as at ERC, the rights may be more symbolic than controlling, but most privately held companies still prefer not to pass through full voting rights. If a company's stock ownership becomes less concentrated, as it has at ERC through public offering and sales to employees, a significant minority share, such as the ERC ESOP, could be powerful if voted as a block. ERC is not concerned about how employees might act as voters. As one of the plan administrators put it, "What's the point of being restrictive? If you really want people to be involved, then do it. The people who work here really understand the issues. Offering voting rights makes the plan work; it's representative of ownership."

Although employees do vote their shares, nonmanagement employees have not yet been elected to the board of directors. ERC added an ESOP coordinator to its staff in January 1984. Employees take all questions and requests for information that relate to the ESOP directly to the coordinator. The coordinator also functions as the center for the daily administration of the ESOP and as the primary contact with the trustee as well as providing staff support to the ESOP committee.

How Employees Evaluate Their ESOP

In 1982 the National Center for Employee Ownership (NCEO) completed a survey of ERC employees to determine their attitudes toward the company and its ESOP. Employees were asked 140 questions dealing with various aspects of their work.

Employees appeared generally satisfied with the company. For instance, on a scale of 1 to 7, employees scored an average of 5.7 on a measure of job satisfaction and 6.4 on a measure of work motivation—somewhat better than scores from other ESOP companies that were studied. Not surprisingly, higher paid employees scored higher than lower paid ones.

Job satisfaction at ERC seems dependent on a number of

factors. Satisfaction with pay, the ability to do significant work and receive feedback on performing that work, employee influence in the company, and support for supervisors and co-workers all rate fairly equally in importance. This suggests that creating a good work environment at ERC requires more than manipulating one or two factors. Employees seek financially rewarding work that allows them to use their skills, influence their company, and interact comfortably with other employees. While it may seem obvious that employees would want these things, the ERC results indicate a relatively higher emphasis on independence and input on the job than do results from other companies. This almost certainly reflects ERC's better-educated workforce.

Also measured were employees' perceptions about their influence in the company. As in almost every company studied, employees would like to have more influence than they think they have. Generally speaking, employees believe they are asked their opinion on some issues and merely receive information on others; they would prefer to be asked their opinion on a greater number of issues and have more of a controlling voice on a few (for issues concerning their jobs, not management-level decisions). On a scale of 1 to 5, employees rate their average influence over a variety of company issues at 2.5 and would like it to be at 3.1. The difference is about average for the companies that NCEO studied.

Finally, data were collected about employees' attitudes toward ownership. Overall, employees were positive about the ESOP, with scores about average compared with other companies that have been studied. The one area in which ERC employees scored higher was in their perception that the ESOP increased their influence in the company. This probably results from the fact that ERC employees can vote their stock.

On a 1–7 scale, employees scored between 4 and 5 on measures of feeling like an owner and working harder because they are owners. In other words, the average scores were just above the neutral point. They averaged 3.8 on questions designed to measure whether the ESOP itself made work more enjoyable. A breakdown of these results clearly shows that ERC employees are positive on items measuring their attitudes toward the financial benefits of the ESOP and less positive on the more attitudinal ones—items such as "I work harder on my job because I own company stock".

The results are consistent with the emphasis ERC has placed on the financial benefits of the ESOP. In fact, employees at most ESOP companies react similarly, and most companies stress the financial side of the plan.[2] It is unclear whether this is cause and effect, however. It may be that employees simply do not react as strongly to the nonfinancial aspects of ownership as they do to the financial ones.

Conclusion

ERC is a good example of using the ESOP as an employee benefit plan. The ESOP was specifically created to provide employees an opportunity to participate in the financial success of the company. As with many new and growing firms, ownership sharing is one of the most practical, sometimes one of the only financially feasible, means of doing so. As ERC has grown and flourished it has sought additional ways to involve employees in the company. The ESOP is now one of several financial and participative opportunities offered to employees.

Employees have reacted to the ESOP much as the company hoped: They see it as an important financial benefit. The company's success with the ESOP as a motivational tool has not been complete, however, since employees would like more opportunities to participate as worker-owners in their company. Fortunately, this seems to be the direction in which ERC is moving.

Perhaps the most important lesson of ERC is the need to reevaluate constantly the role of the ESOP in the company and to design new ways for using the ESOP to meet the changing needs of the workers and abilities of the company.

QUAD/GRAPHICS: CREATING A CULTURE OF OWNERSHIP

W hat is meant by the question, "How well is employee ownership working?" That often depends on who's asking the
question, because different people have different goals and expectations for employee ownership. As a matter of federal policy, for
example, the primary objective of employee ownership is to broad-
en the ownership of wealth. But over the years advocates of the
concept have articulated a variety of additional, coincident goals for
employee ownership, among them democratizing corporations,
improving workers' job satisfaction, and creating a more efficient
economy. As the cases in this book show, individual companies
have used employee ownership to achieve some or all of these
purposes.

For instance, the Lowe's Companies employee stock ownership plan (ESOP) (Chapter 13) is principally an employee incentive and benefit program. Although Lowe's employees vote their
shares, the company does not consider employee ownership to be
the basis for broadly participative workplace democracy. On the
other hand, for the members of the Common Ground Restaurant
Cooperative (Chapter 14), democratic decisionmaking is a top
priority. But the Common Ground hasn't created any bus boy
millionaires. Is one of these companies more successful than the
other? Not really; each is looking for something different from
its ownership plan.

What is distinctive about Quad/Graphics is that it is asking
for so much from employee ownership. Quad is building an en-

This chapter is based, in part, on previous work by Karen Young.

tire corporate culture around the idea that employees are, ought to be treated as, and ought to behave as owners. It is an ambitious undertaking that challenges all the conventional wisdom of the way the United States has traditionally done business. And the results, as we shall see, have proven Quad/Graphics' efforts well worthwhile.

The Quad/Graphics Philosophy

Quad/Graphics is one of the nation's fastest growing and most financially successful printers. It counts among its customers *Newsweek, Harpers, Inc.,* and *U.S. News.* Founded in 1971 by a group of ten printers and businessmen. Quad now employs more than 2,000 people and has sales of over $170 million. At the center of the company's corporate philosophy are Quad's employees, or "partners" as they are called:

> *Our emphasis is not on the numbers, but rather on people who are caring and sharing in common values and attitudes; people who have stretched their minds and broadened their horizons to bring printing from the craft of the Middle Ages to the technology of the Space Age; and people—ordinary people—who have achieved this extraordinary result through the Quad philosophy of people helping people to become more than they ever hoped to be.*[1]

This eloquent philosophy makes Quad/Graphics sound more like a friend, teacher, or family than an employer. And indeed, Quad employees, managers, customers, and even competitors use words like trust, teamwork, sharing, and responsibility to describe the company. By almost any measure, what Quad is doing seems to work. The company has achieved a 50 percent compound growth rate each of the last ten years. It is a leader in high technology color gravure printing. Its employees are among the most satisfied and committed ever studied by the National Center for Employee Ownership (NCEO). What is Quad/Graphics doing to make employee ownership work so well?

44

The Corporate Culture

Imagine you are the newest of Quad/Graphics' 2,000 employees. You've just arrived at the Pewaukee, Wisconsin, headquarters, a luxurious printing shop not far from Milwaukee. According to Harry Quadracci, company founder, president, and "philosopher-in-chief," you are now in "boot camp."[2] You are assigned a mentor, a more senior employee who helps you acculturate into the company, and over the next two years you and the company will decide whether you are right for the Quad/Graphics "family." Quadracci describes the process: "They get indoctrinated, brainwashed—theirs is not to reason why. It's authoritarianism all the way, until they've proven they're adult enough to handle a participative management style."[3]

As a new employee you will complete a rigorous education program at Quad/Ed, a division of the company located in a former school building. Quad/Ed does not hire professional instructors, but rather taps the talent of the company's own workforce and produces its own texts. Quadracci himself teaches the introduction to printing course.

The courses at Quad/Ed are in great demand. In 1983 and 1984 more than 600 employees a week attended classes, over 50 percent of the workforce at that time. According to the company, interest is strong because employees realize that the knowledge they gain prepares them to take on additional responsibility. Quad/Graphics' 1984 annual report described the company's commitment to education:

> *At the core of Quad/Graphics' corporate culture is the belief that the company's competitive edge is not predicated just on buildings and equipment, or even on technology, but in the knowledge and experience of its employees.*
>
> *Passing one's knowledge on to those who come after is an integral part of Quad/Graphics. This precept flies in the face of printing industry tradition—and most journeyman trades for that matter—that says that knowledge is something to be guarded. Quad/Graphics doesn't believe*

45

that by sharing knowledge it puts its own position in peril.

The circle of life at Quad/Graphics revolves around education. An employee's first duty is to learn his or her job, then to know it, improve it and lastly to teach it to the next person who comes after. The cycle continues as the employee goes on to yet another skill.

This process ensures Quad/Graphics with a continuous flow of new ideas. This unique approach has also allowed Quad/Graphics to fulfill its promise of providing employees a method for improving themselves professionally.[4]

Although Quad/Ed provides formal classroom-style training, as a new employee much of your learning will be on the job. Employees are treated responsibly and expected to act that way. They are given considerable latitude in their work, including the usual groups meetings, minimal supervision, and promotion from within typical of highly participative companies. It is not uncommon for new employees to feel a bit overwhelmed at first in this sink or swim atmosphere.

Sometime during your first year you will take part in perhaps the most dramatic example of Quad/Graphics' trust in its employees: the annual "spring fling." Once a year all the managers go off on a day-long retreat, leaving the rank-and-file employees to run the company. Quadracci points out that this is not simply an empty gesture. A lot could go wrong that day: An ad could be misplaced, a machine run improperly, a customer turned away. But the spring fling is a visible symbol of Quad's trust in its employee-owners.

On a more practical, day-to-day level, employees are encouraged to participate in decisionmaking and to take on new responsibility. Employee peer groups, for example, are empowered to set disciplinary standards; once, in fact, a group fired an employee whom Quadracci would have retained. Another time, a group of pressmen appointed themselves to the task of training junior pressmen and imparting their high standards by developing a curriculum and holding classes. Again, Quadracci was never consulted and only learned about the program much later.[5]

This nascent training course eventually evolved into the extensive Quad/Ed school described above.

In a 1983 cover story *Inc.* dubbed Quadracci's style "management by walking away." *Inc.* described the time Quadracci asked the company's truck drivers whether they could haul something back in their empty returning trucks. "When the truckers asked what they should take on the back hauls, Quadracci shrugged, 'How should I know? I don't know anything about driving an 18-wheeler.... I'm not going to find you your loads.' With that, he turned and walked away."[6] The truckers, who previously had little or no business skill, did find loads, and now trucking is one of nine semiautonomous divisions of the company, each run as profit centers by groups of employees. They keep their own records, compete independently for contracts, and even sell to other printers.

Managers and titles do exist at Quad/Graphics but, says Quadracci, not to "give orders." Organization charts are disdained and any employee group can talk to any other, somewhat like the "lattice" structure made famous by another employee ownership company, W. L. Gore Associates. It all adds up to what one employee termed a "scary" level of responsibility, at least until you get used to it. But Quadracci says the company should be a place where people can be more than they think they can be, not just what their supervisors might expect them to be.

The Quad/Graphics Ownership Plan

Along with all of this responsibility, of course, the employees at Quad/Graphics are also owners. Quad established its ESOP in 1974, partly as an employee benefit plan, partly as a way to buy out the interests of the founding owners, but mostly because employee ownership was a part of Quad's philosophy of giving employees a "stake in the company and in themselves."[7]

Since 1974 Quad/Graphics has made significant contributions to its ESOP each year, averaging about 10 percent of each employee's pay since 1980. Today the plan owns 37 percent of the company.

Employees wait one year before they participate in the ESOP, and then wait another three years before they begin vesting. Vesting is completed after ten years. When employees leave they receive the cash value of their ESOP accounts. Although it is a private firm, Quad/Graphics prints an outstanding annual report, which it distributes to employees each year. These reports detail financial information and describe company operations with a candor few companies ever show their employees.

Quad/Graphics also provides a variety of other benefits including medical, dental, and eye insurance, a three-million-dollar sports center, on-site college courses, a campground and lodge, and periodic employee dinners. Employees work twelve hours a day for three days a week, with four days off. The change from the traditional eight-hour day, five-day-a-week schedule raised productivity by 20 percent.

As noted at the beginning of this chapter, Quad/Graphics' employees were among the highest scorers ever surveyed by NCEO.[8] On measures of organizational commitment, in fact, they were the highest. These measures asked employees to agree or disagree with statements such as "For me, this is the best of all possible organizations for which to work" and "I am proud to tell others that I am part of this organization." On a scale of 1 (strongly disagree) to 7 (strongly agree), Quad employees' average response was nearly 6.

Quad employees also reported that they were very unlikely to leave the company; they were, NCEO found, the least likely of any employees studied to look for a new job. They were also among the most satisfied with their work in general and the company's ownership plan in particular.

Conclusion

Quad/Graphics has all the elements of a successful ownership plan. It makes large annual contributions to its ESOP, and clearly the employee-owners have done well with their stock.

Management is thoroughly committed to the idea of ownership and provides ample opportunity for participation. The company continually renews the feeling of ownership, not only by providing financial information, but by treating employees as responsible partners and providing them with significant corporate perks. The result is very highly motivated workers and, the company would point out, an enviable bottom line.

More important, Quadracci insists, the company is a place where work can be fun. The elaborate annual reports stress that characteristic. The 1984 report, for instance, focused on the circus theme at the company's annual bash, a party replete with clowns, a stage show, circus animals, and other trappings. At the party Quadracci suggested that the clown was a good role model for employees to emulate. "People should be more spontaneous," he said. "Overthinking has destroyed more creativity than it has ever solved problems. Ready, fire, aim!"

PHILLIPS PAPER CORPORATION: PARTICIPATIVE DECISIONMAKING

As an employee at his uncles' company, Gil Phillips had observed his fellow workers' lack of concern for the company's goals. He assumed their indifference was the result of close family ownership and family decisionmaking at the company. How, he wondered, could workers become better motivated and more interested in their work? During his younger years he had developed a populist idealism and had read about Yugoslavia's experiments with a labor-managed economy.[1] He concluded that certain features of this system could be adapted to conform with U.S. capitalism and American workers.

In 1973 Phillips put himself in a position to test his ideas when he bought Phillips Paper Corporation from his four uncles. These uncles had formed the San Antonio company as a partnership twenty-eight years earlier. The company is a statewide distributor of packaging products, mostly to food processors and the fast food industry.

Phillips got to work transforming his company right away. In 1973, in his words, he put together a combination stock purchase/stock bonus plan "to insure to each employee a proportionate share of the growth of the company and the security of partial ownership and control of the economic entity on which the employee is dependent."[2]

Parts of this chapter are based on a case study written by Romona L. Ford.

The Plan Structure

Full-time employees become eligible to participate in the stock purchase plan after two years. They may purchase five shares for every $1,000 they earn in compensation, and if they do not have enough cash for the shares, employees may purchase them through payroll deductions. The company offers these shares at 85 percent of book value.

To encourage employee ownership and reward people for staying with the company, Phillips created the stock bonus plan. The bonus plan gives employees ten shares after their fifth, tenth, fifteenth, and twentieth years of continuous employment. The federal government does not tax these bonus shares because it considers them an award from the company, provided the value per employee is less than $400 per year.

Phillips Paper Corporation also has a profit-sharing plan that distributes 7.5 percent of annual profits at Christmastime. In 1983 the company decided to begin distributing an additional 5 percent of profits so long as it retains a cash surplus. The profit-sharing plan distributes the 5 percent bonus in equal amounts to all full-time employees at the annual stockholders' meeting in April. As another incentive for purchasing stock, if workers buy ten or more shares within two weeks of the April profit-sharing distribution, the company awards them an additional bonus of ten shares.

The stock purchase and stock bonus plans have no vesting schedules; employees receive all rights to their shares immediately, except that they must retain ownership of bonus shares for at least two years. Phillips does not want outside ownership of the company, so when employees leave they must either sell their shares back to the company at the current book value or sell them to other Phillips employees. While they are still at Phillips they may hold their shares, sell them to the company at book value, or sell them to other employees.

In addition to the ownership and profit-sharing plans, the company offers employees many other benefits including a pension plan, a personal loan plan, a car payment plan, and tuition reimbursement for work-related education. Phillips also pays wages that are between 10 and 40 percent higher than the median wage for similar work in the area.

The Diffusion of Ownership

The bylaws of Phillips ownership plans state that no employee, with the exception of the vice-president/treasurer, may hold more than 5 percent of the company. By 1984 thirty-one of Phillips' forty-two employees had accumulated a total of 18 percent of the company and the vice-president/treasurer had purchased another 10 percent. Gil Phillips was somewhat disappointed with the slow diffusion of stock ownership—18 percent in ten years—and became concerned with a new trend of employees cashing in their shares.

During the first eight years of the plan workers purchased considerably more shares than they sold. In the ninth and tenth years they reduced their purchases, but net purchases were still positive. However, in the third quarter of 1984 the company was running a net selling balance as many of the long-term employees sold their shares at current value, making a substantial profit. According to Phillips the employees are using the proceeds for family expenses such as higher education for children or a swimming pool in the backyard.

Phillips says that this development has enhanced the morale and commitment of employees and has made newer employees enthusiastic buyers. At the same time, however, the selling trend has slowed the rate of transition of ownership. So in order to turn over a larger percentage of the company to employees, Phillips added an employee stock ownership plan (ESOP) to the company's ownership plans in 1986. By 1986 the employees held 20 percent of Phillip's stock.

Participation Features

For Gil Phillips, having employees own stock and share in the profits was not a substantial enough change in the company.

Following his Yugoslavian example, Phillips gave workers an important role in the governance of the firm. The Phillips Paper Corporation board of directors, which makes decisions by majority vote, is controlled by the employees. The board membership includes Phillips, two other company officers, and six nonmanagerial workers, elected by the stockholders. Workers also have a majority of seats on the five-person committee that administers the employee ownership plans: Two of the members are company directors and the other three are employees, elected one at a time by a plurality vote of all employees.

The board of directors and the ownership plan committee deal mostly with long-term policy matters. Phillips has also set up job committees that handle the firm's daily operations. The job committees, similar to quality circles, cover four functional areas: sales, office staff, warehouse and local delivery, and statewide delivery. Each committee includes all workers in its functional area and meets as needed to discuss scheduling, equipment maintenance and purchase, record keeping, working conditions, and other work-related issues. To keep the atmosphere open and nonthreatening, company president Gil Phillips does not attend job committee meetings, except when invited.

Job committees elect chairpersons who run meetings and report majority decisions to an operations committee made up of two company officers and each chairperson. The operations committee has authority to make decisions in all matters suggested by the job committees. The board of directors may overrule decisions of the operations committee, but it has never done so. In addition to the operations committee, a management committee consisting of five nonmanagerial employees meets when needed to make policy and decide on nonoperational matters such as vacations, sick leave, special events, and companywide household questions. The actions of this committee may also be amended by the board of directors. Finally, all five trustees of the pension plan are also company employees. Phillips believes the plan has no need for outside advisers because the majority of the pension funds are used to finance personal, auto, and home improvement loans to the plan participants.

54

Communication has never been a problem at Phillips Paper Corporation. Because the company is small, Phillips is able to discuss the plan personally with new employees, and everyone receives company financial and long-range planning information.

The Results

Phillips believes his experiments with worker ownership and participation have been successful, and the National Center for Employee Ownership (NCEO) survey results support him.[3] Workers at Phillips reported a composite 5.85 score for job satisfaction—high on NCEO's seven-point scale and significantly higher than workers at other employee-owned companies NCEO has studied. The responses of workers who participate in the Phillips ownership plans indicate that participants are more satisfied with their jobs than nonparticipants, and in general the more stock people own, the more satisfied they are.

Although NCEO has no data on employee attitudes before 1973, Gil Phillips says that he has noticed a marked improvement in workers' attitudes toward their work and toward the company since the days when his uncles practiced a more traditional management style. NCEO interviewed six workers personally, all of whom were unfailingly enthusiastic about the company. "My friends can't believe that there is a company which gives its workers so much opportunity and benefits. They've never worked anywhere like that."

But employee ownership and participation plans do not transform worker attitudes on their own; they require the commitment of senior managers. Gil Phillips introduced the plans to the paper products company, and the workers credit him as an exceptional leader. "His door is always open." "He is the most fair person I've ever worked for." "I might have got mad and quit a long time ago if it wasn't for him."

The Bottom Line

Have all the positive changes at Phillips Paper Corporation made for positive results? Apparently so. Although a strict analysis of the exact cause is not available, Phillips is five times more profitable than before the 1973 changes. Sales per employee are higher than in any of the publicly traded companies in its industry. Retained earnings have increased from 0.5 percent to 2.3 percent of sales. The increase in retained earnings is particularly encouraging because it suggests that management and workers are keeping a careful eye on reinvestment.

As an employee-owned firm Phillips is difficult to classify. The company is neither a worker cooperative nor an ESOP (at least not before 1986), but it does incorporate some of the features of both. Like a cooperative, Phillips maintains a highly participatory governance structure; like many ESOPs, the company is relying on stock purchases to effect a gradual transfer of ownership from an existing owner. What is clear is that Phillips Paper Products is one of the success stories of employee ownership. In the last ten years Phillips has upgraded the worklife of its employees, given them a stake in the company's future, and improved its performance in the marketplace.

6

HYATT-CLARK INDUSTRIES: BUYING A COMPANY TO SAVE JOBS

In August 1980 General Motors announced that it was closing the Clark, New Jersey, plant of its New Departure Hyatt Bearing Division. The plant, which employed 2,000 people, made tapered roller bearings, primarily for large rear-wheel-drive cars. As the market for rear-wheel-drive cars declined, especially in the recession, the need for Hyatt's product declined as well. Moreover, Hyatt had been a difficult plant for GM. Labor relations had always been tumultuous and adversarial. The United Auto Workers contract at Hyatt was, from the workers' standpoint, one of the best in the country, with wages fifty to seventy-five cents per hour above other UAW contracts, and with work rules that kept employment high. In fact, according to shop chairman Jimmy Zarello, the rules "helped create an atmosphere where people who were in the plant eight hours did four hours of work." "That," Zarello said, "was appropriate when GM was making billions in profits."[1] The union's job, under those circumstances, was to keep as many people working for as much money as possible.

From GM's point of view, however, the union's success was management's failure. If Hyatt had been regarded as a profit center, it would have shown losses for years. Other suppliers could supply GM with the parts it needed, and no one else showed an interest in buying the plant. Closing seemed the logical alternative. To GM's employees, of course, it did not seem logical at all. Union president Jimmy May had been reading about employee ownership and decided the idea was worth a try. At first, he recalls, when he suggested the idea, people looked at him "as if he were from Mars." In time, however, May's idea became increasingly attractive.

The first step was to commission a feasibility study. May also arranged for a vote to take $35 from each worker's paycheck, but the proposal was rejected 794 to 778. At this point, local managers added their efforts to the buyout. They leafleted the plant gates on a cold morning—an action that impressed the workers as a sign of management's faith in the idea. A new effort to raise $100,000 from $100 employee contributions succeeded, and the managers and employees hired Arthur D. Little to conclude the feasibility study.

The feasibility study indicated that Hyatt could make a profit if workers took a 25 percent pay cut, work rules were changed, and benefits were reduced by 50 percent. It was a bitter pill, but workers saw little choice but to swallow it. The national office of the UAW, concerned that the concessions might become a pattern and that Hyatt had no future anyway, remained neutral on the buyout.

Hyatt's employees now faced the task of raising enough capital to get the new company started. For that, they turned to GM. A buyout would save GM many of the considerable costs associated with closing—pension, insurance, severance pay, and so on. It would also send a message to other plants. The Hyatt union leaders contended the message would succeed only if GM were to turn over ownership to the workers, which the company would be unlikely to do in most cases. Finally, it would be good publicity. GM thus agreed to purchase $10 million in preferred, nonvoting stock in the new company as well as $13 million in loans to provide a $100 million, three-year purchase guarantee. That helped leverage $15 million in loans from Prudential and $15 million more from other private sources. The money was borrowed through an employee stock ownership plan (ESOP), meaning that 100 percent of the common stock was held in the ESOP trust, to be released to individual employee accounts as the loan was repaid.

Setting Up the New Company

In 1981 the new firm, Hyatt-Clark Industries, was underway. Its workforce had been pared to 800, down from 2,000 before the buyout. Negotiations over how to structure the new firm, however, had been difficult. The union wanted to have employee control; the attorney putting the deal together insisted that banks would not loan the new company money if that were the arrangement. As a compromise, the union was allowed to have three of the thirteen seats on the board, two of which would go to union officers and one to a designated outsider, while three seats would go to management. Respected area businesspeople filled out the board. Employees would not be able to vote their shares until the loans were paid off in 1991. The union also wanted equal distribution of stock and was able to prevail on this point.

In addition to the stock, employees were given a productivity incentive bonus plan and a semiannual profit-sharing plan. As promised, work rules were changed, contributing to an 80 percent increase in productivity. There were also a number of changes in plant layout. Under GM, machines were crowded tightly together, forcing workers to walk around long rows of them to get to the other side. Entire banks of machines depended on the smooth operation of elevators to which they were connected and frequent breakdowns caused serious productivity problems. At the employees' suggestion, the machines were spread more widely, with more elevators per machine bank. The result was an increase in productivity and a more livable workplace. Employee suggestions also led to the creation of an in-house machine shop where previously untaped employee skills were used to rebuild machines and, in one case, design a new one that eventually would be sold outside the plant. Finally, a previously automated assembly operation was, at the suggestion of employees, made manual. This "low-tech" solution actually made much more efficient use of workers' time, increasing productivity by 50 percent in that area.

Participation Programs

From the outset, one of the goals at Hyatt was to increase employees' involvement in the organization and control of their work. In addition to the design considerations mentioned above, a variety of employee participation programs were set up.

Initially, a series of skill-building sessions was established for middle and lower management. The sessions provided training in employee ownership and quality of worklife programs. A council was also created to deal with the concerns of salaried workers. Twenty specially trained workers were designated to deal with production and other problems as they arose. Symbolic distinctions, such as executive dining rooms and reserved parking for management, were eliminated. All of these efforts reflect the desire to create a more democratic atmosphere.

On the more day-to-day side, a series of productivity teams was established. Workers meet regularly in small groups to discuss various problems, propose solutions, and then post them in common areas. These groups are organized in much the same way as qualitity of work life teams elsewhere. What is significant at Hyatt is that they are part of a larger effort of other programs to involve and reward employees, not just an isolated process within traditional ways of doing things.

Finally, a series of roundtables was established. Four times a week ten hourly workers meet with the president, Howard Kurt. Participation is voluntary and employee participants are self-selecting. Any subject can be discussed. Kurt sees the roundtables as a major contributor to company performance, generating important new ideas and creating positive employee peer pressure. Union leaders May and Zarello are more skeptical, seeing the roundtables as a means to circumvent the unions. At one point they urged members to boycott the meetings, but they have since determined that they are "purely voluntary."

Union Participation in Management

May and Zarello were named to the board, and in addition, union representatives attend weekly management staff meetings. May and Zarello clearly see their role on the board as representing the union. "The responsibilities are the same," May says of his dual union/board function. "I'm responsible to my members." Still, he believes that in an employee-owned company, "unions have to be more realistic—we can't afford to go in to management and demand certain things, because the company would be bankrupt within five years."

May nonetheless characterizes his role as "adversarial," and the board meetings have reflected some continuing hostility and distrust on both sides. Zarello contends that Kurt is "very reluctant to get union and hourly workers involved in top management decisions." Board chairman Allen Lowenstein, the lawyer who set up the ESOP, argues that May and Zarello still feel a need to "zing" management at each meeting. For his part, however, Kurt maintains that "the beautiful thing about employee ownership is that the more people understand the finances and problems, the easier your job becomes."

The battling that goes on in the boardroom seems atypical of the general experience with employee representation on boards, an experience the National Center for Employee Ownership's own management survey results indicate has been very positive. In companies where employees elect the board, every management official surveyed reported that the practice was a positive factor in the company. Hyatt's charged atmosphere appears to reflect the extremely adversarial relationship that was traditional there. Still, it seems doubtful that either side would want to eliminate union representation on the board.

Success and Problems

The revival of the economy, and especially the increase in sales of large, rear-wheel-drive automobiles, helped Hyatt to meet its economic goals ahead of schedule. With productivity up 80 percent and labor costs down significantly, Hyatt was able to report a small profit in 1983 and also to pay off $6 million in interest charges. Employment has increased from 800 at the time of the buyout to 1,500. Certainly in terms of the major purpose behind the buyout—saving jobs—Hyatt had been a great success.

There are still important issues to be resolved, however. GM is renewing its contract with Hyatt, but the continuing shift to front-wheel-drive vehicles and the ever-present possibility of oil shortages make Hyatt's primary market uncertain at best. The company has not made the progress it hoped in finding new products or new markets, although it is still working on these problems.

The union leaders still feel that participatory management has not yet arrived, although they acknowledge some progress. May says that supervisors and middle managers continue to affect an authoritarian attitude toward employees. Salary issues are a source of conflict, as they have been from the outset. The union wants to see a flattening of salaries, while management insists that moves in this direction make it hard to retain and attract top management people. Recently, the issue became a major problem. Management refused to disclose salary figures, so the union threatened to sue over the issue. Management then agreed, and when the workers saw the increases managers received they were furious. Many management people received increases well above the fifty cents per hour that workers had received both in absolute and percentage terms. May and Zarello wanted management to limit its increases to the increases workers received; management said this ignored the sacrifices management had made and continued to make relative to what they might earn elsewhere. In the end a merit system was set up to replace the wage increases, and management received an average 5 percent increase. The conflict, however, soured relations on the plant floor, and productivity dropped sharply.

While these problems are serious, they can be seen as part of the process of changing from a very traditional, authoritarian, bureaucratic, adversarial system to a more democratic and participatory one. Both sides had a lot invested in the old ways of doing things. By contrast, in many nonbuyout situations, labor relations are often more harmonious from the beginning. It can be argued that these companies would be more likely to set up such plans to begin with or, at least, they have more time for a gradual transition than exists in a buyout.

Employee Survey Results

In 1983 the National Center for Employee Ownership (NCEO) performed a survey of Hyatt employees. Although many of the results cannot be released, since the company has requested that the data be treated anonymously, some of the primary findings can be discussed.[2]

Generally, the survey revealed that Hyatt employees were quite positive about the plan. Eighty-seven percent agreed that "owning stock in this company makes me more interested in the company's financial success." Seventy-eight percent of the hourly workers and 61 percent of the salaried workers agreed that "because of employee ownership, people here try to cooperate more." Over half of the workers (52 percent) say that employee ownership makes them want to stay with the company longer.

For most workers the key variable in explaining their feelings about being owners at Hyatt is how much influence they believe they have in the company. This is in contrast to most other companies we studied where the financial benefits were the most important factor. Hyatt was also the only distress buyout we studied, however. Most Hyatt employees did not believe that ownership has given them the greater say in how the company is run that they had hoped for. While this seems to fly in the face of obvious increases in worker input (e.g., seats on the board, the roundtables, and the participation programs), it is not uncommon in buyout situations for workers to react this way. Expectations are raised considerably, and these expectations can rarely be fully met. Moreover, Hyatt's employees do not yet have voting rights on their stock, and the union's leaders have been very critical of management. Finally, every company NCEO studied, even the most thoroughly democratic ones, shows a gap between workers' perception of their current influence and the level of influence they would like to have. As Hyatt's participation efforts mature, and as workers eventually gain voting rights, one would expect this gap to narrow.

Conclusion

Hyatt's experience with a worker buyout illustrates many of the difficulties such an effort entails. Raising capital, in itself a problem, may necessitate compromises that employees or managers are unwilling to make. Reestablishing markets and creating new, successful products is a challenge for any company, let alone one in which disinvestment has often been going on for years. Buyouts, almost certainly much more than other kinds of employee ownership efforts, create much greater expectations among workers about their new role in the company, particularly if they have made sacrifices to make the buyout possible. Some of these expectations are unrealistic; some need time to be realized; others are frustrated by management's expectations that things should not change. Arriving at a workable compromise between everyone's expectations and the business needs of the company is a difficult challenge.

Yet, as the NCEO survey indicates, few people at Hyatt regret that they have made the effort. Existing jobs have been saved and new jobs have been created. Conflict remains, but many innovative solutions have been found as well—solutions that have improved productivity dramatically and provided workers with specific, concrete ways to have more input into corporate matters.

Postscript

After the NCEO study relations between labor and management deteriorated considerably over conflicts about whether to distribute new profits, how to interpret an earlier profit-sharing agreement, how much new investment was necessary, and how to increase worker participation in the company. In 1984 this led to substantial reverses for the company. The board subsequently approved a new plan for corporate governance after much research. Unfortunately, neither the company's economic situation nor its labor-management relations improved. In the fall of 1985 Hyatt declared chapter 11 bankruptcy and the chairman announced that the company would seek a buyer. Initial efforts to do this fell through, but workers then agreed on a new contract with new concessions. The concessions were expected to keep the company open until a buyer could be found or the company's fortunes improved.

Some might question whether the sale of Hyatt-Clark would be a failure of employee ownership. But it should be remembered that the buyout's principle objective—saving jobs in a company in which traditional ownership and management had given up—would be largely achieved.

7

THE SOLAR CENTER:
REFLECTIONS OF A SOCIALIST
ENTREPRENEUR

In 1975 Peter Barnes decided to become what he called a "socialist entrepreneur." As a former editor of *The New Republic*, he'd flung his share of arrows at the big corporations, but inwardly he feared they were invincible because no one else could deliver the goods—the cars, stereos, and bananas—we'd grown so accustomed to consuming. If the Left rejected corporate capitalism, he reasoned, it had to come up with some workable alternatives and a body of people who could carry them out.

To be sure, he could see a few problems. First there was his general innocence about business matters: "I'd never deciphered a financial statement, much less met a payroll." Second, there was the matter of startup capital, an "especially sticky wicket," Barnes noted, "when (a) you aren't rich, and (b) you believe that labor should control capital, not the other way around." Finally, there was the whole question of how to embody noncapitalist philosophical values in the actual operation of a business. He liked to think of himself, quietly, as a democratic socialist, but he had only the vaguest notion of how democratic socialism might work in practice.

He decided there was only one way to find out: to learn through experience and overcome obstacles as they arose. So, along with five like-minded individuals, he founded a business called the Solar Center.

This chapter is extracted, with permission of the author, from Peter Barnes' unpublished manuscript.

Today the Solar Center is a modestly successful firm employing twenty-five people, all of whom are owners or on the track to becoming owners. The company has found a market niche—central solar water-heating systems and cogeneration systems—that makes economic sense in urban and suburban San Francisco. Sales have reached $2 million, and the employee-owners earn a respectable income. Internally, the company is democratic, but its structure has changed significantly over the years. This chapter traces the history of those changes and records the lessons Barnes would pass on to other small, democratically managed, worker-owned businesses.

The Early Years

"In retrospect," Barnes recalls, "our naivete in those early days was astounding. Our marketing ideas were, to put it benevolently, eclectic." They thought they would sell a little of everything—solar greenhouse kits, do-it-yourself "breadbox" water heaters, photovoltaic toys, books, consulting services—and that their biggest problem would be turning away the thousands of solar enthusiasts who would beat a path to their door.

Their notions of how the business would operate were equally romantic. Barnes doubted that they'd have to buy a truck or rent a warehouse; he would simply lend the business his pickup and they'd use a friend's garage for storing things. In addition, they would rotate jobs and take a month off every summer to run rivers together.

Needless to say, this was not exactly the way things turned out. Still, Barnes recalls, their eager innocence was in many ways a blessing, for it spurred them through myriad obstacles that "would have deterred even the shrewdest capitalist." And for about three years the founders of the Solar Center did lead a kind of dreamlike existence. They worked hard but exuberantly for poverty-level wages; they played and socialized after work; they even rafted some spectacular rivers in the mountains of Idaho and northern California.

Eventually, though, the dream ended and the business began in earnest. The Solar Center pioneered several ingenious ways to finance large solar hot water systems for apartment buildings. They learned how to manage commercial-scale projects costing hundreds of thousands of dollars, how to use cranes and computers and subcontractors and tax shelters. They moved from a small office and warehouse to an 8,000-square-foot building with drive-in access for their six trucks.

Ownership

From the beginning what most clearly distinguished the Solar Center from more traditional businesses was ownership. While technically a stock corporation, the Solar Center was founded on the principal that ownership should be tied to labor. This was not just an abstract idea. It was rooted in the belief that people feel better about their work if they own what they produce, own the tools they use, own and control their workplace—in short, if they work for themselves.

Still, ownership is not a simple thing. It has its rewards, but it also involves risk, sacrifice, and patience. People at the Solar Center believe that owners must make an investment—they must put something *in* before they can get anything *out*—and they must be prepared to defer taking out for an unpredictable period of time.

The founders of the Solar Center think that at first they underestimated the importance of sharing risks. They invested $5,000 apiece and countless hours of unpaid time. Newer workers, who hadn't made the initial investment, tended to want maximum short-term pay, while the founders focused on long-term viability.

For several years they went back and forth about whether new employees should be required to make a cash investment in the business, and if so, how much. Eventually, despite much hesitation by employee-owners who had gotten aboard for free, they agreed on a required minimum investment of $3,000. This amount was substantial enough to help the business and to be felt as a risk by owners but not so large as to be prohibitive. To enable workers without savings to become owners, the Solar Center adopted a payroll deduction plan that allows the investment to be spread over two years.

The Solar Center also had to grapple with the problem of how, in an ongoing business, new owners would be admitted and old owners disposed of. The process of becoming an owner involves a formal meeting with current owners at the end of a one-year probationary period. At these meetings there are frank discussions of job performance, levels of commitment, and the meaning of ownership. When a new owner is accepted he or she begins purchasing stock, becomes eligible for profit-based bonuses and additional stock distributions (from an employee stock ownership plan—ESOP), and is entitled to vote for and serve on the elected board.

Before an employee became an owner and made an investment it was always understood that he or she could be fired, but there was confusion about whether the company could fire people *after* they became owners. In fact, the members of the Solar Center shared a strong bias against firing or laying off owners, partly because they believed in giving people chances to redeem themselves, partly because, as a worker-owned business, they felt more obliged to preserve jobs than to earn profits, and partly because they were simply afraid to fire people.

Over time, however, they came to accept the reality that becoming an owner in a small, thinly capitalized business could not guarantee lifetime employment and that firing people directly—after honest evaluation and due process—was better than the inevitable alternative of firing them indirectly through disrespect and pressure to resign.

To be sure, getting fired was a rare way for people to leave the Solar Center. More commonly, despite the incentive to stay and help make one's investment rise in value, owners over the years voluntarily chose to move on to other activities. Whatever their reasons for departure, the Solar Center had to develop a method for "cashing out" existing owners without decapitalizing the business. They accomplished this through an ESOP, which they established in 1978. When owners leave, the ESOP redeems their stock at its book value but spreads payment in monthly checks over four years, with interest on the deferred portion. The departing owner thus receives an income stream that is paid for in part out of investments by incoming owners and in part out of the ongoing cash flow of the business.

Power

At the Solar Center managers are workers who specialize in managing. They have day-to-day authority over workers who specialize in other things, but they are also accountable to those workers, who retain the authority to make many basic policy decisions. The result is a kind of circular power structure.

But it was not that way at first. When they started the Solar Center the founders did not foresee the power-related problems they would encounter or the workable solutions to them. According to Barnes, their ignorance was blended with an idealistic sixties-type faith in participatory democracy: "We thought it meant lots of meetings, with decisions made by consensus of all participants, and a loose organizational chart which allowed people to perform a variety of tasks."

They ran the business according to that philosophy for about three years, and for most of that time it worked well. One key to this success was that the core group members were all dogged workers who trusted each other implicitly. Another was that they rigorously held policymaking meetings on unpaid "owner's time" after regular working hours. This preserved daily productivity and helped keep meetings short and business-like.

Eventually, however, their consensual democracy began to break down. At staff meetings an individual or small minority would object to a policy or personnel decision and prevent or delay the forward motion of the business. In daily operations people who had responsibility for "getting things done" would feel frustrated by their lack of clear authority. Barnes remembers:

*At the time, we were greatly perturbed both by the per-
sonal anguish these problems often caused, and by the
feeling that some noble ideal had failed. In retrospect, it
became clear that our experiment in consensual democracy worked well when we were small, cohesive, and zeal-
ous, and began to sputter after we added people with different viewpoints and clashing ambitions, and got tired of
so many meetings. Nothing ignoble was involved in this
sputtering; it simply reflected our need for a more sophisticated structure that blended our democratic values with
new operational realities.*

So, instead of the weekly staff meetings at which a multi-
tude of decisions were made, they cut back to monthly staff
meetings that are primarily informational. Twice a year now,
they have full-day staff retreats at which goals for the following
six months are set and major issues—such as growth, structural
changes, and compensation policy—are discussed.

At other times direction of the company is in the hands of
an elected board, which hires (and can fire) a chief executive
officer. The CEO, in turn, hires (and can fire) department heads,
who are responsible for running their departments in accordance
with overall business objectives. Their operating philosophy
became: If someone is responsible for getting something done, he
or she must have the authority necessary to carry out that
responsibility.

These changes were adopted over time and amidst grum-
bling that, as worker-owners, they were disenfranchising themselves and becoming a more heirarchical, management-run organization. In fact, they did become more hierarchical and
management run, but after the initial shock wore off almost
everyone agreed that the business ran better and that the Solar
Center had not abandoned democracy but shifted from direct to
representational democracy—not the distant kind associated
with political institutions, but a much more intimate kind in
which the elected representatives were co-workers who were actually at the shop every day.

Money

At first the founders thought that all workers should receive the same compensation. Installers, salespeople, engineers, administrators—they were all equally valuable, equally dedicated, and equally worthy of reward. The debate that raged in the early years was whether some workers should receive more than others on the basis of need, which was primarily defined by the number of children a worker had.

As time passed, however, it became evident that some people were working harder, had greater skills, or could command more money on the outside than others. There was also a problem of motivating salespeople; some were more productive on commission than on salary. Eventually they developed a compensation policy based on the following principles:

1. Pay differentials were justifiable based on skill and performance, but no member of the enterprise could receive more than two times what other members received.
2. Installers would be paid hourly, office people monthly, and salespeople on commission, but wages, salaries, and commission schedules would be designed so that comparable performance received comparable compensation. In other words, an excellent installer would receive approximately the same as an excellent salesperson, while an apprentice installer would earn less than an experienced installer.

Distribution of profits was a less controversial subject, perhaps because for many years there were no profits to distribute. The worker-owners never doubted that profits, despite their capitalist connotations, were a good thing. While not an end in themselves, profits were needed for the company to survive as a corporate enterprise, to build a cushion for hard times, and to provide an opportunity to grow. When they finally recorded a profit after five years, the worker-owners' sense of pride was palpable, and the issue of how to distribute profits moved to the fore.

Committees were formed to consider the various options. The entire staff then met one evening to decide the final profit-sharing formulas. The discussion was orderly, and the decision was responsible and fair: 70 percent of the profits were to be retained in the business, 25 percent distributed to the workers, and 5 percent given to progressive community groups such as a center for battered women and a food program for the needy. The amount the worker-owners distributed to themselves was divided according to the formula: one-third based on months worked during the year the profit was earned; one-third based on total months worked; and one-third based on cash invested. This split, they reasoned would equalize disparities in regular compensation, reward people for their "sweat" investment during unprofitable years, and provide an incentive to cash investment. Barnes recalls the decisionmaking about profit sharing:

> *What was more significant than the actual formulas was the sheer phenomenon of the debate itself—the act of a group of workers sitting down at the end of a year and deciding how to divide the fruits of their labor. I remember thinking to myself how extraordinary this scene was, how unthinkable within the context of capitalism as we know it, yet how logical, how satisfying, how right! In a very real sense, this was what socialist entrepreneurship was all about.*

The Lessons

In his "Reflections of a Socialist Entrepreneur" Barnes drew five lessons from his experience for those interested in starting a democratic, worker-owned business:

> 1. *Growth is inevitable, so accept it, plan for it, and enjoy it. No matter how much you want to stay small and informal, there is an economic and psychological dynamic that pushes even worker-owned businesses to*

grow—first in size, and then in formality of structure.

One of the ironies of our experience was that every time we discussed growth in abstract terms, we agreed it would be nice to stay small; yet every time we had to make decisions affecting sales volume, salary levels, and job descriptions, we made choices that led to cautious growth. Our motives were not to maximize return on invested capital, but to achieve financial stability, to do things (like research and development) that weren't inherently profitable but made our work more interesting and less hectic, to increase our incomes, and to give owners an opportunity to take on new challenges and responsibilities.

2. *Democratic organizations need leaders, and leaders need to be supported and rewarded.* A business enterprise, whether socialist or capitalist, needs an entrepreneur—someone whose job it is to envision new possibilities, to inspire others to make commitments, to unite scattered resources, to scan for opportunities and dangers, to guide, goad, promote, protect, learn, teach, trim, and hold together.

   A socialist entrepreneur should be paid well, but the primary rewards must be intangible: recognition from peers, the excitement of translating ideals into realities, the joy of watching other people learn and grow. If there are to be more entrepreneurs with socialist values, society as a whole must develop nonmonetary ways of training, supporting, and recognizing them.

3. *Authority must be matched to responsibility.* Putting it more colloquially, if you want somebody to do something, you have to give him or her the authority to do it. It is amazing how long it took us to accept this simple concept, how deeply ingrained was our resistance to empowering individuals. We learned the hard way that failure to follow this rule did not make us more democratic—it just made us more inefficient and frustrated.

   As a matter of practice, managers given authority to

perform or supervise a task will, within a democractic environment, consult others who are affected by their decisions. But they can and should be responsible for making the decisions. The test of a democratic structure is not how many decisions are collectively voted on, but whether managers themselves are ultimately accountable to the employee-owners.

4. *Never forget to make the organization—and its values— self-renewing. This dictum would be true of any organization with a desire for longevity, but it is especially true for cooperatives in a capitalist melieu. Because the larger society is continuously broadcasting counter-messages, a cooperative enterprise must consciously build— and vigilantly maintain—mechanisms for renewing its internal esprit de corps.*

   One crucial mechanism involves risk-taking. Requiring new owners to make an investment comparable to the previous owners' is probably the best way to do this.

   Another crucial aspect is intergenerational yielding. There is a tendency for the founders not to pass on power to the second generation, for the second generation not to pass it on to the third, and so on. For a cooperative to remain a cooperative, its leaders must consciously welcome new generations into positions of ownership and responsibility.

   A third aspect of self-renewal is education. New employees in contemporary America will rarely have experience in cooperative business practice. It is important that they be "socialized" and brought up to speed in systematic ways, including seminars on the company's history, finances, and structure.

5. *Get sophisticated, not cynical. Things are not always the way we would like them to be. Compromises have to be made. People have conflicts when we wish they wouldn't. Utopia is not around the corner.*

   Faced with these realities, we have two choices: We

can get cynical and bitter, throw up our hands and say that our ideals have failed; or we can get smarter and more sophisticated, learning new ways to approach problems without surrendering our fundamental beliefs.

Conclusion

The National Center for Employee Ownership surveyed employees at the Solar Center in 1982 and found that they were very satisfied with their jobs and committed to the organization. On measures of satisfaction with their employee stock ownership plan, Solar Center employees scored higher than employees at any other ESOP company we have ever studied. They also reported both the highest level of employee influence in decisionmaking and the greatest satisfaction with their influence over decisionmaking.

Peter Barnes, cofounder of the Solar Center and president for five years before leaving to begin promoting other cooperative business development with the Industrial Cooperative Association, is not surprised at the Solar Center's high scores:

During seven years in the solar industry, I watched many capitalist businesses come and go. By contrast, our little "socialist island" turned out to be remarkably sturdy. In part this was due to luck, in part to some good business decisions, but in part it was also due to our structure. We had less turnover, more creativity, and more commitment from our workforce than did most of our competitors. When the going got tough, our worker-owners hung in there—because their jobs, their investments, their baby, were at stake.

Postscript

With the expiration of the federal solar tax credits in 1985, much of the solar industry entered a severe recession. The Solar

Center, now with a reduced staff of twenty, is looking for new markets, including cogeneration.

8

ALLIED PLYWOOD CORPORATION: THE SECOND GENERATION OF OWNERS

W hat happens to a successful small business when the founder retires and turns it over to the employees? This is a question more and more business owners and workers are asking as employee ownership spreads across the United States. The answer is important because no one wants to see a company fail, neither the owner who has spent a lifetime building it nor the employees who depend on it for their jobs. And it is no wonder people worry that when the entrepreneur has gone, maybe the entrepreneurial spirit will go, too.

But Allied Plywood is one employee-owned company that has put these worries to rest. In the three years since the founders completed transferring their stock to the company's employee stock ownership plan (ESOP), Allied has boomed. The company's financial success has brought enormous satisfaction to both the workers and the former owners.

Allied's success is more than financial, however. Today the company is a model for the smooth transition from traditional ownership and management to employee ownership and democratic participation. Before they retired, Allied's original owners resisted relinquishing control of a business they had worked for years to build. But as they gradually sold their stock to the ESOP they trained the workers to take their place. Now employees routinely consult with managers on company policy and investment decisions. Allied's efforts to draw out the entrepreneurial spirit in all of its thirty employees have resulted in high profits and satisfied workers.

Deciding on Employee Ownership

In 1975 Phyllis and Ed Sanders began to plan for their retirement. For the previous twenty-five years they had been pouring their hard work and sharp business sense into Allied Plywood, and within a decade they would be ready to turn it over. But to whom? The Sanders had no heirs interested in running the family business and, like so many retiring owners in this position, Ed and Phyllis were facing one of the most difficult decisions of their careers.

The couple had founded Allied Plywood in 1951 with less than $10,000. Ed remembers how hard it was at first:

We started up in an abandoned coal yard. I built a little wall for the weight so that you'd at least have a little area to drive the trucks under and weigh them. Before it had just a small roof there. I bought a freight car load, and we just started from there. She'd help me load the truck and go out and deliver it. It was a tough start. It was real tiny at first and then it just grew and grew.[1]

By the middle of the 1970s Allied Plywood delivered to a market area with a thirty-mile radius around Washington, D.C. Company sales were in the millions. Despite this success, the Sanders still had a problem: "You know, the company grows every year, but your wallet's the same size. The money isn't there to spend and enjoy, but the stock is worth more and more." In order to realize the benefits of the company's growth the owners would have to sell.

The Sanders had three options: They could have the company buy their stock directly; they could sell to another corporation; or they could set up an ESOP at Allied and sell to it. Each of these possibilities received different tax treatment from the U.S. government. Whatever the Sanders chose, it would have sig-

80

nificant consequences for both their checkbook and the future of Allied Plywood.

The first choice, selling Allied stock directly and gradually to the company, would be the least desirable. Such a sale would be subject to ordinary income tax, which was 70 percent at the time. Now it is 50 percent.

Financially, the second option was more attractive. If a company bought Allied for cash, only capital gains tax would be due—a maximum of 28 percent then, 20 percent now. At the time, however, the government gave even more favorable tax status to small business owners who traded their companies not for cash but for stock in acquiring corporations. The government did not tax owners on the gains from this type of transfer until they eventually sold their shares of the acquiring corporation, perhaps years later. This tax law created a perverse incentive for owners to sell to conglomerates and, in fact, a number of large syndicates did offer to buy Allied. Ed Sanders knew the financial advantages of selling to one of these firms:

> *I could take my stock and Boise Cascade or somebody could just make an exchange of stocks, and then I'd have no tax to pay. I'd be in their company you see. I'd get their dividends. I could sell a few shares of stock, just speak to my broker on the telephone, quickly, easily.*

The decision to sell was more than an economic one, however. To Ed and Phyllis Sanders the idea of their company being swallowed up by a corporate giant was not appealing. Their years of hard work had bonded their identity with the company. But what really kept the Sanders from selling to a large corporation was their sense of loyalty to Allied's employees. The Sanders fan a benevolent business with generous employee benefits, and they were afraid a new corporate owner would forget about the workers. They carefully evaluated the decision as Ed Sanders states:

> *Well, it's mainly from my obligation to the people that have been here for so long. [I] couldn't see it. We have a*

bonus set-up, and I could see that going down the drain in a hurry. . . .

If another company merged or bought it, well, all they'd do is sit back and look at the balance sheets and the profits [and] losses. And that's all they care about. And they hire somebody with a whip from someplace to come in . . . and straighten it out. And then all they do is look at profit, top and bottom. That's the way they work. They even advertise it.

Some of these big conglomerates have thirty different divisions. And they're going to buy and sell here . . . and sell the ones that are losing money and buy five that are in a sympathetic industry. I know the way they are.

So, the Sanders chose not to sell to an outsider. In 1976 they learned about the tax advantages of an ESOP from a letter to the editor of the *Washington Post*. The letter pointed out that an ESOP could buy the shares of a retiring owner and the owner would only have to pay capital gains taxes on the sale. The company makes tax-deductible contributions to the ESOP and the ESOP uses the money to purchase stock from the owner. In terms of taxes, transferring ownership to an ESOP was not as beneficial as swapping stock with a corporation, but it was considerably better than selling stock directly to the company.

The Sanders decided it was worth paying the extra taxes in order to preserve the integrity of Allied and to give the employees a share of the ownership. But they were unhappy about the more generous tax treatment for conglomerates. Over the next several years Ed Sanders became a vocal supporter of comparable tax incentives for ESOPs. It was Sanders who first suggested the idea that sales to an ESOP be treated as favorably as sales to a corporation. Partly as a result of his efforts, Congress changed the law in 1984 and made ESOPs the most tax-favored means for owners to sell their businesses.

For retiring owners, selling to an ESOP is now even better than swapping stock with a corporation. After selling 30 percent or more of a company to an ESOP (not 80 percent as required with another company), an owner can roll over the gains on the sale by reinvesting in the stock of other companies. No taxes are due on the transfer until the owner subsequently sells the new stock, at which time only capital gains taxes are due. Although it came too late for the Sanders, the 1984 tax law provides some of the most significant legislation encouraging employee ownership.

The Allied Plywood ESOP

The Allied ESOP performed admirably as a mechanism for converting the Sanders' assets to cash. But the Sanders did not decide on an ESOP merely to liquidate their holdings; employee ownership fit nicely into their style of doing business. For years Ed Sanders had been looking for new ways to get the employees more involved in the company and to begin to identify their own fortunes with those of the company. Previously he had tried to sell stock directly to the workers. But these efforts failed because workers generally had little extra money for what they considered luxury items like stock. Through the ESOP employees became shareholders at no personal expense.

The Allied ESOP got underway in 1976. At first the ESOP was not leveraged, that is, it did not borrow money to buy stock. Instead, the company made cash contributions each year, equal to about 24 percent of payroll, and the ESOP slowly bought the Sanders' stock, accumulating about 60 percent of the company by early 1982. That year Phyllis and Ed Sanders retired and the ESOP arranged a loan to purchase their remaining shares. The company, then fully employee owned, finished paying back the loan in 1984.

All full-time employees participate in the Allied ESOP. Vesting occurs over a ten-year period, with 30 percent vesting after three years and an additional 10 percent per year thereafter. Allied allocates shares according to employees' total compensation. The company wants to ensure that all employees share in the ownership, so Allied is planning to continue issuing stock to the ESOP even though the company is already 100 percent employee owned. They can do this by printing new shares, which dilutes the value of existing shares but does not change the value of the company. That way, new employees will become owners too.

Allied does not want the workers to leave still in possession of their shares because then the company would no longer be 100 percent employee owned. Therefore, when workers leave or retire they must sell their vested shares back to the ESOP at book value. The company has begun setting aside a fund for repurchasing retiring employees' shares.

Allied paid employees dividends on their shares until 1982, when the ESOP borrowed money to buy the last of the Sanders' stock. While the company repaid this loan it gave no dividends but, with the completion of loan payments in 1984, Allied may begin passing through dividends once again. Passing through dividends is one of many ways Allied reminds workers of their ownership in the company. Allied also distributes financial reports to employees, and each year it gives employees reports on their ESOP accounts (which are printed on stock certificate facsimiles). The ESOP reports show individual employees the transactions in their accounts: the balance at the beginning of the year; company contributions; redistributions; dividends; and end-of-year balances. The stock certificate facsimile (see Figure 8–1) is symbolic of the attitude at Allied that workers are not just "beneficial" owners but real owners of the company.

Allied also has an outstanding cash profit-sharing plan. Each month the company contributes a certain percentage of the month's profits to a bonus pool that it then splits equally among all employees, from the president to the fork lift drivers. At the end of every year each employee receives an additional bonus. The year-end bonus is not split equally but is somewhat discretionary. In determining the size of each employee's year-end bonus, the company considers seniority, days worked that year, job class, and performance.

The profit-sharing plan has a number of advantages for the company. Because bonuses vary according to profits, the plan helps the company adjust its payroll to the cyclical and seasonal

> ⟩ **ALLIED** ⟨ **PLYWOOD** ⟩ **CORPORATION** ⟨
>
> **EMPLOYEE STOCK OWNERSHIP PLAN**
>
> *REPORT OF ESOP ACCOUNT BALANCES FOR YEAR ENDING SEPTEMBER 30, 1978*
>
> TO:
>
> Social Security Number
>
> | | STOCK BONUS PLAN | | | MONEY PURCHASE PLAN | | |
> |---|---|---|---|---|---|---|
> | | Company Stock Account A | | Other Investments Account A | Company Stock Account B | | Other Investments Account B |
> | | Number of Shares | Original Acquisition Cost* | Present Value | Number of Shares | Original Acquisition Cost* | Present Value |
> | Your Account Balance at Beginning of Year . . . . | | | | | | |
> | Your Share of Company Contributions and Reallocated Forfeitures . . . . | | | | | | |
> | Your Share of Other Transactions Involving Acquisition of Stock During Year . . . . | | | | | | |
> | Your Share of Dividends and Other Trust Net Income (Loss) . . . . | | | | | | |
> | Gross Account Balance at End of Year . . . . | | | | | | |
> | *Minus:* Cash Dividends Paid to You . . . . | | | | | | |
> | *Minus:* Withdrawals. . . . . | | | | | | |
> | Your Account Balance at End of Year . . . . | | | | | | |
>
> As of September 30, 1978, the book value of Allied Plywood Corporation stock was $229.86 per share, making the present value of the _____ shares of company stock in your ESOP accounts worth $ _____. Adding this to the other investments held in your ESOP accounts, the present value of all your ESOP Account Balances totaled $ _____
>
> Based on your employment date of _____, you accumulated _____ years of credited service by the end of the year, so that your vested interest (non-forfeitable share) in your ESOP Accounts is _____%.
>
> *Reflects the sum total of the acquisition cost of all shares of company stock in your ESOP Account at the time they were originally contributed to or purchased by the ESOP Trust.*

Figure 8–1

building industry. Profit sharing also provides Allied's employees with pay that is about one-third higher than employees of the company's competition. Allied has not missed a monthly bonus payment for eight years, and sometimes the monthly bonuses are as high as $1,000 to $1,200 per worker. Finally, profit sharing has a tendency to equalize ESOP stock allocation. This is because the ESOP allocates stock according to total compensation, including bonuses, and monthly bonuses are equal for all employees.

Allied's current president, Bob Shaw, considers it important to have a profit-sharing plan in addition to the ESOP since profit sharing gives employees an immediate indication of the company's performance. Profit sharing is a prominant part of Allied's overall compensation system, which emphasizes employee ownership and rewards employees for company performance. Indeed, workers at Allied do not receive high wages, but they more than make up for it with monthly and annual bonuses, dividends, and stock ownership. Ed Sanders has reported that in good years warehouse workers at Allied could earn over $40,000 in compensation over and above their ESOP accounts.

Informal Participation

Because Allied is a privately held company, voting rights do not have to be passed through to the employees on their shares. But federal law requires that employees be allowed to vote their shares on major issues such as a merger or liquidation. Sanders reluctantly surrendered these limited voting rights but did not like the idea of handing over control of his company. If the law had required him to pass through voting on all issues, he says he may not have opted for an ESOP:

> *If we were to have the vote pass through on all that stock that they have, here I'd be with half my life's work invested, with minority say in what I'd had full control of. I think a vote pass through is fine once my interest had worked down to be somewhat like theirs.*

Sanders also considered voting stock inappropriate for a company the size of Allied:

There's a big difference between twenty employees and two hundred. They're entirely different situations. So many of the problems at Allied Plywood are small, and if you were to have to vote on them, you'd use up so much time that it would just cost too much to do it.

As president of the company, Ed Sanders preferred an easy-going management style. For example, Allied held periodic employee meetings after work as often as people seemed to think they were needed. When the ESOP was new the company had meetings once a month; at other times they were quarterly, or even yearly. According to one employee, the workers would simply close the doors and get together to talk about suggestions, ideas, gripes, and problems. In recalling these meetings, one employee said,

We'd stay for a couple of hours and we'd review the ESOP, and then we'd all have a chance to rap and say what was on our mind about the company and why we didn't like this and that and the other. They go ok, but some people just won't say anything, and some people just say the same things over and over. You get twenty people there and one guy wants to talk about how his truck's not running.

Employees were also somewhat reluctant to speak up at company meetings. The same worker says:

The meetings overall go fairly well to air our opinions and our gripes. I think people may hold back things. Again, you got a group of twenty people there with Mr. and Mrs. Sanders and they don't want to say what's on their minds.

Sanders, too, was ambivalent about the meetings and eventually came to feel that they were too formal and that "nothing

87

came of them." Shortly before he left Allied he discontinued the meetings.

Still, Sanders was genuinely open to employee suggestions. Often, when workers thought they had a better way to do things, they would go to his office to discuss it. Another worker says: "The Sanders have got an open door policy that just won't quit. It really is an easy sounding block. You can say pretty much what you want and change things. The system is pretty good to us, so we don't want to make too many changes."

But changes were coming. This employee was speaking in 1980; two years later the Sanders would retire. The workers had become accustomed to good, paternalistic owners. While things were going well they had not worried about questions of participation, voting rights, and control. Sanders felt an obligation to his workers, and they had deferred to his leadership and experience. But what would happen when Sanders was gone and the employees took over complete ownership? One person's words echoed the feelings of many: "There are people who say when the Sanders leave it's going to be chaos, the place is going to fall apart. . . . Because it can't run without them."

New Forms of Participation

In 1982 Bob Shaw, a long-time company employee, succeeded Ed Sanders as Allied's president. Like Sanders, Shaw has a relaxed management style and the workers seem to trust him. Shaw says he would not do anything the employees did not want him to, even if he felt they were wrong.

Since becoming president, Shaw has noticed that Allied's employees are beginning to think of themselves more like owners. They do not want to be told what to do unless they know why, and sometimes they just stop working and start asking questions. Such behavior might have driven Frederick Taylor to smash his stopwatch on a nearby pallet of plywood. But Bob Shaw did not study at the school of scientific management. "It can be frustrating," he says, referring to the work time lost, "but fortunately I was a schoolteacher before coming to Allied. They're not stupid, you just can't talk over their heads." Shaw explains Allied's operations to the workers, knowing that once a job makes sense to them the company can save considerable time and money.

Bob Shaw is not the only one explaining things at Allied these days. Recently the workers did some explaining of their own when they wrote evaluations of each other. The employees did not hesitate to include the company president in their written comments, which, according to Shaw, were not all rave reviews. "I learned some things about myself," he says with a smile, "and I'll try to make changes."

The company has formalized its participation structure since the Sanders left. Allied Plywood now has a seven-member board of directors, five of whom are company employees. Shaw and vice-president Gene Scales serve on the board as company officers, and the workers elect the other three employee board members. Each worker has one vote and workers elect, one at a time, one board member from the office/sales staff and two from the warehouse. After the first board election in 1982 Shaw was pleased that the employees had chose good, "hard-working" representatives. The company attorney and company accountant are the other two board members. Shaw thinks it is necessary to have nonemployees on the board in order to get outside opinions. The employee owners have also reinstated the company meetings. They had planned to have meetings every month but decided to hold them less often because Allied was doing so much business that employees were working until seven or eight o'clock at night and were too tired to stay for meetings.

Shaw expects that Allied will eventually pass through full voting rights on ESOP stock, but he says that for the time being the company is too busy selling plywood to go through the legal work involved. At this point the action may seem a mere formality anyway. Employees already elect workers to the board of directors, and they have a vote on major issues, which Allied defines very broadly. For example, workers recently held a vote on whether to buy a new $70,000 computer system.

Employee Attitudes

The National Center for Employee Ownership (NCEO) surveyed employees at Allied Plywood early in 1982. The respondents indicated that they were quite satisfied with their jobs, scoring an average of 3.94 on a five-point, five-item scale. Only 11 percent of the workers said they would be looking for a new job within a year, compared to 30 percent of the respondents in a 1977 nationwide survey asking the same question. Indeed, turnover at Allied has been very low. From 1951 to 1980 only one person quit.[2]

The survey results show that employees are very interested in and pleased with their ESOP. More than 90 percent disagreed with the statement, "I really don't care about the employee stock ownership plan at this company." And more than 70 percent said that owning stock in the company made them more concerned about the company's financial success.

Only 39 percent of the Allied employees responding thought that they had more influence in company decisionmaking because they owned stock. This may be because employees participated in decisionmaking to a limited degree even before they owned stock. But also, NCEO surveyed the employees before the Sanders had retired. Now that they hold 100 percent ownership, elect board members, and vote on more issues, they may have different feelings of control.

For instance, in 1982 the average Allied employee response on a question about worker influence over company hiring was 1.8 on a scale from 1 (no say) to 5 (workers decide). But since the company has been fully employee owned the employees have actually voted to rehire a worker who had left Allied to start a business with his father in Florida. If workers are now making important personnel decisions themselves, their impressions of worker influence, over hiring decisions at least, may be different.

Conclusion

When the Sanders announced their retirement plans five years ago, some of Allied's employees were worried about the future of the company. But they have no doubts now. Allied Plywood is flourishing under employee ownership. Sales increased 20 percent in 1984 and 25 percent in 1985, topping 16 million. Moreover, the employees are involved as never before in the financial benefits of ownership as well as the governance of the firm.

Allied is a textbook example of gradual social change. Had the company rushed into full employee ownership and democratic participation, the transformation may not have succeeded. The ESOP structure allowed the Sanders to pull out their equity slowly, and the fact that they did not have to pass through full voting rights gave them the sense of security that, as business founders, they desired. The employees, too, needed time; they had to adjust to their new roles as employee-owners.

As the workers have started to participate more and more in running the firm, they have probably learned the truth in what Ed Sanders once said about being the boss: "You know, you always have the feeling some jobs are more glamorous until you get into them." Sanders was right. Working ten-hour shifts to run the business they own may not be glamorous, but for the entrepreneurs of Allied Plywood it certainly is rewarding.

9

FASTENER INDUSTRIES: TRANSFERRING FAMILY OWNERSHIP TO EMPLOYEES

Fastener Industries is a 125-employee manufacturer of industrial weld fasteners—nuts, bolts, and other fasteners that are welded onto automobiles, refrigerators, computer cabinets, and hundreds of other kinds of metal equipment. The company was founded in 1905, and in 1928 the family of R. J. Whelan gained control and maintained ownership until mid-1980. At that point the family members holding stock decided to sell the company. Richard Biernacki, then treasurer of the company (and now president), suggested an employee stock ownership plan (ESOP) as a means to buy out the shares of the president and the other family members still holding stock.

The idea appealed to the Whelan family. They could get the cash, fair-market value for their stock, the company would continue as an independent firm, and the employees would become owners. Since there had always been a good relationship between the owners and the employees, including a generous profit-sharing plan, that last point was a particularly important consideration.

Transferring Ownership to the Employees

When the decision was made to sell the business a number of options were considered, including finding outside buyers. With twenty-one people owning stock, it was no simple task to find a solution with which everyone would be happy. The ESOP option, however, was just that solution.

In order to purchase the stock, the company first sought to convert the assets of the profit-sharing plan into an ESOP. Individual employees were given the right to decide whether to transfer their interest in the profit-sharing plan accounts into a new ESOP trust account that would invest in company stock. All but six opted for the ESOP plan. Since some of the employees lived out of state, a special filing with the Securities and Exchange Commission was necessary.

These funds, along with a bank loan taken by the corporation, provided the money necessary to purchase all the outstanding stock in the hands of the selling family, leaving the ESOP as the only shareholder. As the company repays its loan it contributes as much stock as it can under the law (generally 25 percent of payroll) and deducts the value of the contribution from its taxable income. The sellers paid capital gains taxes on their gain from the sale of stock.

The procedure used at Fastener, it should be noted, is not the one most companies in this situation would use. Normally, the company would simply contribute earnings to an ESOP, which the ESOP would then use to buy out the shares of the owner. This process would take place over several years as the owner phased into retirement. The company could deduct its payments to the ESOP, and the owners would defer taxation altogether or pay at most a capital gains tax on the sale, which would be much lower than the ordinary income tax on an installment sale. If the owner wanted to get out all at once, the ESOP (or the company) would borrow the money, with the company making tax-deductible contributions to the ESOP to enable it to repay the loan. In effect, this would allow the company to deduct both interest and principal on the loan, not just interest.

In Fastener's case this could not be done because the law at the time too strictly limited the amount a company could contribute to an ESOP to repay a loan. Those limitations have been substantially eased, however. The need for an SEC filing is also unusual, having arisen because Fastener was both converting a profit-sharing plan and, in effect, asking employees who lived out of state to buy company stock with their share of the plan's assets.

The additional legal expenses were considered well worthwhile. The initial bank loan for the purchase was negotiated without any problem, and, after the first year, the bank lowered the interest rate. Fastener's long and solid record made the ownership transfer entirely practical from the bankers' perspective.

Designing the ESOP

Fastener's ESOP provisions are considerably more liberal than those of most ESOPs. All employees are eligible to participate after one month of service and become immediately vested once they are in the plan. According to the company's president, Richard Biernacki, this quick enfranchisement was to prevent employees' staying with Fastener simply to gain seniority and thus accumulate more stock. Most companies, by contrast, require gradual vesting both to encourage employees to stay and to reward those who do. For reasons that will become apparent, however, turnover at Fastener is very rare.

Employees also have full voting rights on their stock. As a closely held company, Fastener could have lodged most voting rights, in effect, with management. Biernacki had read about problems at South Bend Lathe, where workers owned 100 percent of the stock, but management controlled how the shares were voted. A year before Fastener became employee owned, employees at South Bend Lathe went on strike. Biernacki was convinced that "if you don't vote the stock, you don't really own it."[1] Moreover, he felt that if he, as president, could not convince his shareholders that what he was doing was in their interest, then he was not doing his job properly.

When employees leave the company they can take the stock or its cash value. If they choose the stock, they have a fifteen-month period during which they can ask the company to buy it at its fair market value. If they hold it after that period, they can sell it elsewhere (although it would be hard to find a market), but the company has a right of first refusal. Since the law provides a number of ways for employees to minimize the tax they pay on this stock, the company has provided for four hours of free consultation with the company's attorneys of CPAs to determine the best strategy for each employee.

Stock is allocated to employees according to relative pay. Since the spread between the highest and lowest paid employee is not very large, no employee owns more than 4 percent of the stock.

Worker Participation on the Job and in the Boardroom

Fastener Industries has several formal and informal programs that provide opportunities for employee input into all levels of the company, but it is the attitudes of management and workers that seems to be most important in giving workers a voice in their company. On the management side these attitudes are reflected in a day-to-day willingness to seek out what employees think and to take their ideas seriously; on the employees' side it is reflected in the willingness of workers to make suggestions that merit serious consideration. In the National Center for Employee Ownership of (NCEO) studies of employee ownership companies, in fact, it was determined that the attitudes of management and workers are more important than the formal structures for participation making an employee ownership company open and participative.[2] Biernacki summarized these attitudes well: "It works both ways. He [the worker] owns the place and expects to be involved; you [the manager] respect that he owns the place and you want him involved. You know he knows best; he can save you a lot of problems."

While much of the participation at Fastener is informal, relying on contacts between workers and managers, there are also more formal opportunities. Every six months, for instance, each employee meets in a group of eleven or so randomly selected employees with the president. In other words, Biernacki has about eleven such meetings every six months. The meetings are open to any topic and provide the workers with an opportunity to be heard at the highest level. For Biernacki they provide direct access to what workers are thinking, without having the information filtered through a second or third party. Biernacki was surprised to learn that this technique has a name in management theory—*deep sensing*. It is used primarily as a means for top management to cut through layers of bureaucracy to find out more about their company. Biernacki simply considers it a sensible way to keep in touch with employees.

At the shopfloor level, plant managers meet with employees after the monthly management meetings. Any topics can be discussed, but the primary purpose is to inform shopfloor employees of decisions that management has made. After the ESOP was established, Biernacki recalls, employees wanted to know about what went on in the management meetings, so the shopfloor meetings were instituted. Supervisory personnel also have a number of informal meetings with employees to discuss issues as they arise. When new machinery is purchased, for instance, supervisors consult with the employees who will use the machines.

Finally, the employees elect the board. The board currently consists of five employees, four of whom are from management; the other is the corporate secretary. Anyone can run for the board, and fifteen people did in the first election. The election is held at the annual shareholders' meeting. Biernacki sees the board as directly responsible to the workers and believes it has a responsibility to justify its actions to the employee-owners. The company regularly sends out detailed financial information to all employees.

This high level of employee participation and control does not disturb Biernacki: "I think they [management] realized there would be pressure on them to do what was right and fair, but as I look at it, that's beautiful, that's the way it's supposed to work. When you make a decision you have to have your reasons, and have done what was fair, at least to the majority of the workers, or you are going to be in trouble."

Company Performance

The company became employee owned during the severe recession of 1980 to 1983. Fastener had always been profitable, and it was at least able to break even during this period—a notable accomplishment in an industry in which layoffs and closings were common. During these years the company decided to build an inventory and keep everyone employed rather than lay people off, even though that policy meant reduced profits. Now that the economy is improving, Fastener's profit picture looks very good.

Employees work seven-, not eight-hour days and are paid better than the industry norm. (This does not include the considerable additional sums now in ESOP accounts.) These practices existed before the ESOP and have continued since its creation. These benefits contribute to a very low turnover at the company. Since satisfied employees notify their relatives when openings arise, many workers are related to one another.

Survey Results

The NCEO survey of Fastener employees was completed in late 1983. Overall, Fastener employees had some of the highest scores of any that were studied. On scores of job satisfaction, organizational commitment, and work motivation, for instance, they scored from 5.5 to 6.3 on a seven-point scale, placing them in the top 10 percent of the companies surveyed. As in other companies, an employee's ability to control his or her work and the support received from supervisors showed the highest correlations with job satisfaction and attitudes toward being an owner. Not surprisingly, workers saw themselves as having a relatively high level of input into decisions at the firm, although, as is always the case, they would like to have more. Finally, workers were very positive about the employee ownership plan, scoring in the low to high fives on a seven-point scale on various measures of ownership attitudes. These scores were 1 to 1.5 points higher than in other companies studied.[3]

Conclusion

The transfer of ownership from a retiring small business owner or owners to the employees is one of the fastest growing uses of employee ownership plans. Since the motivation behind such transfers often reflects a happy relationship between management and employees, these companies seem especially good candidates for employee ownership. The increased role employees generally hope to have in an employee-owned company is usually less threatening in such companies, and the very fact of the owner's retirement makes it much easier to amplify employees' voice in management decisions.

Fastener Industries is a good illustration of how successful this approach can be. The company has made a smooth organizational and economic transition to its new ownership, and the result appears to be a more satisfying and a more financially rewarding workplace.

UP-RIGHT, INC.: REDUCING THE RISKS OF OWNERSHIP

W orkers at an employee-owned company are entrepreneurs sharing in the financial risks and benefits of ownership. The benefits can be great, as evidenced by retiring workers taking with them tens or even hundreds of thousands of dollars in equity. But the risks can be equally great, especially in bad economic times. When workers depend on the survival of their company not only for their jobs and income but also for their pension, the stakes can mount to all or nothing. If such a company goes out of business its employees lose both their work and their future security during retirement. Because of these dangers, some risk-minimizing workers might prefer not to become employee owners. But a company in Berkely, California, has designed an unusual package of benefits that combines the advantages of employee ownership with the security of a traditional retirement plan.

Up-Right is a manufacturer of portable and mobile work platforms and mechanical grape harvesters. The company designs, manufactures, and tests most of its products in four company facilities, three in North America and one in Europe. Marketing products to end users, Up-Right generates over 90 percent of its $40 million revenues through company-owned sales offices and rental depots throughout North America, Europe, and the Far East.

Up-Right was founded in 1947 by Wallace Johnson, a man renowned for his many talents. He served as company president through 1978. Johnson wrote several books describing his views on public policy issues, including employee ownership. His last book advocated greater tax incentives for employee stock owner-ship plans (ESOPs).[1]

Johnson did not limit his enthusiasm for employee owner-ship to his writing, but integrated it into Up-Right's corporate philosophy. In 1953 Up-Right established a profit-sharing plan and every year contributed half of all profits over 5 percent of sales. The profit-sharing plan investd half of its assets in Up-Right stock. Under this plan, however, Up-Right had to have cash profits in order to make a contribution, a continual chal-lenge for management.

In the 1970s Up-Right found a solution to this problem. Through his personal contacts with Louis Kelso, Johnson learned that an ESOP would allow Up-Right to distribute a larger per-centage of its earnings to employees. The reason is that ESOPs, unlike profit-sharing plans, do not depend solely on cash contri-butions. While companies may contribute cash to their ESOPs, they may also contribute treasury stock or even newly issued shares. This allows a firm to make both crucial new investments and contributions to an ESOP at the same time. Thus, ESOP employees can share not only in the profits but also in the capi-tal growth of their company.

In 1975 Up-Right decided to convert its profit-sharing plan to an ESOP. The Up-Right ESOP has two contribution plans—a money purchase plan and a stock bonus plan. The money pur-chase plan requires the company to contribute 8 percent of covered participants' compensation to the ESOP each year. Up-Right must make this contribution, regardless of profitability. During very profitable years the company may make an addition-al contribution of an amount up to 17 percent of covered com-pensation to the stock bonus plan, by a sharing of profits from U.S. operations.

Up-Right contributed a total of 20 percent of covered com-pensation to the ESOP in 1978 and 21 percent in 1979. With the recession of the early 1980s Up-Right slowed its contribution schedule, adding the required 8 percent of covered compensation to the money purchase plan and making no stock bonus contri-butions in 1980, 1981, and 1982. Also in the 1980s Up-Right contributed stock rather than cash to the ESOP, which allowed the firm to receive tax deductions for ESOP contributions while conserving cash.

All U.S. employees are eligible to participate in Up-Right's ESOP after one year of work. The ESOP allocates stock according to salary, and ESOP accounts vest at 6.66 percent per year, with full vesting in fifteen years. As required by law in all publicly traded ESOP companies, Up-Right employees vote their allocated shares. But Up-Right has always had a liberal policy regarding employee stock voting rights. Even before going public in 1980 Up-Right passed through the vote on ESOP shares. Moreover, the ESOP committee votes the unallocated shares in the same proportion as employees vote allocated shares, in effect giving the employees voting rights on all ESOP stock.

Uncertain Share Prices and the Pension Guarantee

Company founder Wallace Johnson died unexpectedly in 1979, and a year later Up-Right's management decided to take the company public. Going public helped the Johnson family find a market for its otherwise illiquid holdings. It also relieved the repurchase liability of the ESOP. Now when workers retire they no longer have to sell their shares to the ESOP or the company; instead, they can sell them on the open market. This is good news for the ESOP, which previously had to find cash to buy back retiring employees' stock.

Public trading of Up-Right stock has proven a mixed blessing. Since 1980 the over-the-counter share price has fluctuated considerably, from a low of $5.00 to a high of $10.50 in 1981, $3.50 to $6.50 in 1982, and $5.00 to $9.50 in 1983. The company attributes some of this volatility to the relatively thin market for its shares due to the high proportion of shares held by banks, investment funds, the ESOP, and other large holdings. Because of the relatively few shares on the open market, market forces are amplified or exaggerated.

The uncertainty of the share value concerned many employees who were counting on their equity in Up-Right as a retirement benefit. So in 1981 the company implemented a pension guarantee plan to provide a safety stop to downside risk in the ESOP without reducing the upside potential.[2] The plan establishes a floor for retiring employees' ESOP benefits. Retiring employees receive benefits from the pension guarantee only if the market value of their vested ESOP account is less than the benefit defined by the pension guarantee. Up-Right distributes to its employees a brochure that illustrates the pension guarantee plan.

Pension Guarantee Plan of Up-Right, Inc.

Consider an employee who plans to retire at age sixty-five on January 1, 1983. Assume the employee has thirty years of service and the following partial salary history:

Year	Compensation
1980	$14,900
1981	15,800
1982	17,000

Up-Right computes the employee's pension guarantee as follows:

For service prior to 1981:
  1.2% of 1980 compensation for each year
  of service before 1981 = .012 × $14,900 × 28 = $5,006/year

For service after 1980:
  1.2% of compensation for each year
  1981 = .012 × $15,800 =   190/year
  1982 = .012 × $17,000 =   204/year

For a total of $5,400/year

If the stock value were such that the ESOP account could provide only $4,500 per year, the pension guarantee would make up the annual $900 difference. If, on the other hand, the ESOP account provided $7,000 per year, which is higher than the guarantee, there would be no payments in addition to the ESOP account. Total income per year in these two cases, assuming that social security provides $4,600 per year, is then:

Income Source	Example 1	Example 2
ESOP	$4,500	$7,000
Pension guarantee	900	0
Social security	4,600	4,600
	$10,000	$11,600

Up-Right's pension guarantee plan is an innovative approach to providing employees with the security of a pension plus the upside potential of an ESOP, and it seems likely that a number of other firms will imitate the idea.

Other Plan Features

Since Up-Right employees are scattered among several manufacturing facilities in some forty sales offices across the United States, the company has difficulty communicating the ESOP concept. To meet this challenge Up-Right publishes operations reports and bulletins about the ESOP for employees. The bulletins are in a question and answer format, and the company encourages employees to submit questions on subjects that interest them. Employees also receive proxy solicitations each year for the annual shareholders' meeting. Distributing financial information and proxy forms helps to ensure that employees feel like owners and improve their motivation. The National Center for Employee Ownership (NCEO) studies suggest that it is more effective to disseminate repeated reminders about an ESOP than to make just one, all-out communications effort. Periodic reminders have a cumulative effect, steadily building employees' sense of ownership.

Until 1982 Up-Right had paid dividends on its common stock, although the ESOP did not pass them through to plan participants. Instead, Up-Right allocated dividends to participants' ESOP accounts. Since the company has suspended dividends, it has not benefited from the 1984 tax law that gives an additional tax deduction to ESOP companies that pass through dividends. While there is some recognition that dividend checks would give employees an immediate reward for company performance and would serve as a frequent reminder of their stock ownership, Up-Right managers feel that any dividends paid are more effective for the participants if left in the ESOP.

In most ESOP companies employees cannot withdraw their vested shares until they leave the firm or, in some cases, until they reach retirement age. But Up-Right allows them to withdraw and sell some of their shares while they are still working if they experience a hardship. After five years of participating in the ESOP, employees can withdraw up to 50 percent of their total vested value in the ESOP or their total vested stock bonus plan balance, whichever is smaller. These emergency withdrawals are subject to the approval of the ESOP committee and must be for one of four specific purposes: (1) the down payment on a first home; (2) expenses of a serious illness or death; (3) educational expenses of family members; or (4) living expenses after layoff.

In addition to the ESOP, Up-Right also has a productivity bonus plan for all manufacturing employees. The bonus is based on a productivity factor and a bonus pool factor. Up-Right determines the productivity factor by dividing invoiced shipments by payroll (output/input). The bonus pool factor, a measure of Up-Right's ability to pay a bonus, is a ratio of each facility's actual shipments to its break-even point. Up-Right paid bonuses nearly every quarter for many years, although the recession interrupted payments during 1983 in two of Up-Right's factories because of reduced shipments.

Company Performance

The recession severely affected Up-Right's business. In 1981 the company reported losses for the first time in its history, with a net loss per share of $.87. Profits in 1982 and 1983 were modest—net income per share was only $.21 and $.23—and achieved only as a result of fairly drastic measures. As Up-Right's president Ted Ockels explains in the company's 1982 annual report, "Up-Right management rolled up their sleeves and made a lot of tough, unpleasant decisions. Expenses were slashed. Salaries were frozen. Facilities we could do without were closed." In 1982 Up-Right closed one factory and two rental depots.

These and other measures, along with the upturn in the economy, appear to be paying off. Although profits were still low in 1983, by 1985 they had increased 50 percent. In early 1986 Up-Right announced a 97 percent increase in operating profits for 1985 on a 5 percent revenue increase, an indication that the company is generating a significantly greater return from existing resources.

Employee Attitudes

NCEO surveyed employee attitudes at Up-Right in the summer of 1983. The survey results suggest that Up-Right employees are quite committed to their company and especially supportive of the employee stock ownership plan. Of the roughly 100 employees who responded, 86 percent said they were proud to own stock in Up-Right; more than three-fourths said the ESOP was important to them and that it made them more interested in the company's financial success. A majority of the respondents believe that employee ownership makes their day-to-day work more enjoyable and encourages managers to treat workers more like equals. Seventy-eight percent of the employees said that owning stock makes them want to stay with the company longer than if they did not own stock.[3]

In their written remarks on the NCEO survey, employees commented on everything from the ESOP to particular plant managers. Many comments had a common theme, focusing on the difficult times Up-Right has experienced in the last few years. Although dismayed by the company's recent financial performance and upset by Wallace Johnson's death and the transition to a new management, employees have a certain abiding faith in the company, as this representative comment shows: "Because of our country's economic situation, I don't feel that this is a very good time for a questionnaire such as this one. But considering my company's situation, I feel that we will once again see good times and profits in the near future."

Conclusion

By 1983 Up-Right employees owned nearly 40 percent of the $40 million company through their ESOP, and their share of ownership is still growing. The Up-Right ESOP, of which the employees are so proud, has a number of special employee benefits. The ESOP committee votes unallocated shares according to employees' wishes; employees may withdraw portions of their vested accounts for emergency expenses; and the company has a unique pension guarantee plan to assure employees of a decent retirement. Up-Right is among the nation's most innovative employee ownership companies.

11

WESTERN AIRLINES: TRADING WAGES FOR STOCK

In 1983 Western Airlines embarked on a new partnership—the Western Partnership—with its employees. The plan, designed principally to reduce costs and improve productivity in an era of airline deregulation and increased competition, provides employees with a 32 percent stake in this, one of the nation's largest airlines. In addition to stock ownership, Western's plan provides employees with opportunities for participation in decisionmaking from the job level to the boardroom. Unlike most employee ownership companies, Western did ask its employees for wage cuts in exchange for ownership. This use of employee ownership, trading wages for stock, is a new and important trend in some troubled industries, although it accounts for less than 2 percent of employee ownership plans generally.

Like many major air carriers in the early 1980s, Western was in financial difficulty. By 1983 the company had suffered four consecutive years of losses, totaling more than $200 million. It had not made a smooth adjustment to airline deregulation; it was plagued by very poor relations between unions and management; and both creditors and investors were beginning to regard it as a likely casualty in the airline wars.

In 1983, however, Lawrence Lee was installed as the new CEO, and Western embarked on a program to restore its profitability. Included in the program was a 10 to 18 percent wage cut for employees (10 percent for most workers, 12.5 percent for management, and 18 percent for pilots) in return for 32 percent of the company's stock and two seats on the board of directors. As Western would advertise, its employees at the time owned more of their company than did the employees of any other major airline in the United States. A profit-sharing plan was also instituted, and Western is now in the process of setting up job- and management-level employee participation programs.

This process has been repeated at a number of other airline and trucking companies. Both industries were deregulated, allowing the entry of new, often nonunion competitors into previously restricted fields. The competitors often had lower costs, including lower wage levels. As this was happening the economy was in the midst of a severe recession. Both air travel and freight shipments declined. Many established union companies started losing money—a lot of money. Some simply closed, as did Braniff in 1981. Others, such as Continental Airlines, declared bankruptcy in order to circumvent their union contracts. A number of companies negotiated lower wages for all employees, while some, such as American, set up two-tier wage systems under which new employees were paid substantially less than existing ones.

Western, however, was one of six major airlines (Eastern, Pan Am, PSA, Republic, and TWA were the others) and over fifteen trucking firms (some of which are no longer in business) to negotiate an employee ownership program in return for the wage concessions the company believed it needed to stay in business. It is a pattern that seems likely to continue in these industries and expand to others. By following this approach, companies can give employees something in return for their concessions, often including a say in company affairs. The contributions the companies make in new stock to an employee ownership plan dilute the holdings of existing shareholders but generate a tax break the company can use if it returns to profitability (the contributions are tax deductible). Since the companies would otherwise likely fail, the shareholders can hardly object to this dilution. Moreover, the companies at least hope that the ownership sharing and participation programs will increase motivation and productivity. From the unions' point of view,

110

ownership ameliorates the painful concessions, protects jobs, and gives them a window on the company.

Building Up to Ownership

Western, with about 10,000 employees, is one of the oldest major airlines, with a route system focused on the western United States. Its initial reaction to deregulation was to attempt to strengthen its system by merging with Continental, an effort that ultimately failed. Losses began to mount in 1981, leading to the installation of a new CEO, Neil Bergt. Bergt's primary objective was to merge with Wien Air Alaska, a company in which he had a financial interest. That failed as well. Western had substantial fixed assets (airline gates, planes, and facilities) that could not easily be sold, making it difficult to scale down to the reduced passenger loads it was carrying. Bergt then decided to revamp the company's route structure and with this had some success. But Bergt had brought in all new management, and many of these people did not work out since many did not have experience in the airline industry.

A more serious matter, Western needed concessions from labor. Bergt approached Western's unions (pilots, air transport employees, transport workers, flight attendants, and Teamsters) to ask for the concessions, but they responded by asking for a substantial employee stock ownership plan (ESOP). Bergt was unalterably opposed to the idea. Moreover, while asking for concessions, he gave management a substantial bonus. Predictably, labor-management relations, already not good, became bitter.

In early 1983 Bergt left Western to start a new company, Mark Air (which, ironically, has an employee ownership plan similar to that at People Express). Lawrence Lee, a forty-year Western veteran, was then appointed CEO. Lee had a very different view of employee ownership and was determined to set up a constructive, cooperative approach to labor-managment relations, in contrast to the confrontational approaches being taken elsewhere. Western called in the consultants who had negotiated the ESOP at Pan Am, including Dick Phenneger, a Pan Am pilot and union leader.

The result was the creation of the Western Partnership. Under the partnership employees received 32.4 percent of the company's stock in return for concessions. The stock is held in a special trust. The unions wanted full voting stock, but the company believed that this would make it impossible to win shareholder approval. Employees can vote on major corporate issues such as mergers, tender offers, sale, and the formation of a holding company. They also can elect two members of the board. The company contended that other than board elections there have only been four cases of shareholders voting on anything at Western (mostly on whether to authorize new shares), so voting rights were not all that important. The board, they argued, was where most major decisions were made, and the employees did get representation there. It should be noted that the Western plan is technically not an ESOP but rather a related kind of ownership plan. Normally in an ESOP employees would legally have full voting rights, but the Western plan does not fall under this rule. Since their plan is not an ESOP, however, it cannot be used to borrow money.

Stock is allocated according to the wage concessions made by each group. Given the fact that the concessions came on taxable income, whereas the stock is tax deferred, employees actually received almost as much in after-tax benefits with the stock ownership plan as they would have received in salary.

In addition, a profit-sharing plan was set up. The plan will not be terminated until at least $2 million is distributed in each of two years. Employees will receive 15 percent of Western's first $25 million in pretax profits and 20 percent of pretax profits over $25 million. On a $30 million profit (a figure the company last achieved in 1978) an average employee would receive $475.

Implementing the Plan

The plan itself is governed by a trustee, with a partnership committee acting as a monitor to ensure compliance with the rules of the plan. This committee is composed of representatives from all the employee groups at Western. It is also responsible for communicating with employees about the plan and about the company's finances.

Western makes a very active effort to keep employees informed about the plan. At the plan's inception a series of local meetings was held to explain it, and a partnership newsletter is still sent to all employees to answer questions and explore various aspects of the plan. Toll-free telephone numbers and an address to write with further questions are also provided.

Soon after the ownership plan was started the company began touting it in advertising and sending employees mail inserts they could use for paying their bills and other correspondence. The inserts urged people to fly Western and pointed out that the employees were now owners. A "WOW" (We Own Western) program was created through which employees can volunteer their time for such efforts as sales blitzes.

These essentially promotional efforts are intended to be supported by employee participation programs at both the management and job levels. At the management level this support is basically left to the two employee directors. As of this writing, however, the employee groups have been unable to agree on how to appoint these two people. The Transport Employees want their union president to be on the board, but the Teamsters believe that this would put this person in a conflict-of-interest situation. The Teamsters believe nonunion officers should serve instead. There is no clear legal guidance on this issue from the courts, largely because it rarely came up before 1979. On the one hand, a union official may be seen as the best representative of his or her membership, being the person that membership elected. On the other hand, a union official is supposed to represent only the interests of the employees and could be put in a clear conflict-of-interest position as a board member. There are also a variety of National Labor Relations Act (NLRA) and antitrust law questions about a union official serving on a board.[1] To avoid these problems, the Teamsters and others have argued that representation on the board should be provided by someone who does not hold a union office and who is elected or appointed by the employee shareholders.

Once this issue is settled the two employee directors will serve both as conduits for information about the company to the employees and as a means of making employee-generated policy suggestions to the board. This latter function, if it is to be effective, will require some kind of mechanism for generating and condensing these ideas. At other companies with employee representation on the board, an employee steering committee is often established for this purpose, typically acting as an intermediary between employee participation groups at the job level and the board of directors. Western, however, is still determining whether it will follow this approach.

At the job level the company is committed to setting up some kind of employee involvement program but has not yet decided on its structure. As a first step, however, they have hired a team from Boeing to train middle management to assume a more participatory style. The theory here is that employee involvement programs often fail because of the resistance of middle managers who fear or resent a perceived loss of authority. By training these managers first, Western hopes to avoid such problems later.

Conclusion

Western's program is too new to evaluate, other than to report that labor and management are committed to the effort and believe it is essential to the company's future. The concessions, originally made for only one year, were extended into 1984, and by early 1985 the company had returned to profitability. In fact, the company made its first profit-sharing distribution in 1985. Western believes that the new plan will improve productivity and motivation, and perhaps even attract customers, but that remains to be studied.

What can be said at this point is that the Western approach is no longer unusual. The rapid growth of the stock for wages bargaining pattern, along with the profit-sharing and employee participation programs that generally accompany it, are transforming much of the airline and trucking industry and may well spread to other industries as well. If these plans work, they will almost certainly provide a new and significantly different model for labor-management relations.

12

THE WORKERS' OWNED SEWING COMPANY: SELF-HELP AND WORKER OWNERSHIP

Poverty in the United States is an intractable problem. For years government strategists have devised programs to combat the causes and the symptoms of poverty. We have tried macroeconomic approaches, both conservative and liberal. We have tried trickle-down policies to stimulate investment and "lift all boats" and comprehensive support systems to patch up the victims of destitution. Despite our best efforts, however, the number of poor people in this country is growing. As policies have replaced one another without achieving victory, frustration has grown with government's apparent inability to conquer poverty.

In the last several years a handful of small groups have turned to employee ownership as a new weapon against poverty. None of these groups believe that employee ownership alone will overcome poverty, but they do see certain features in the concept that make it good artillery in some circumstances.

First, when workers own their own business, profits stay in the community either as personal income for the worker-owners or as investments in the company for future income. Employee-owned firms have no absentee owners collecting the returns to capital. Second, workers have an economic incentive to work harder when they own their business. The more productive they are, the higher their earnings. Finally, when poor people become employee-owners they take a first step toward economic inden-

---

This chapter draws heavily on a previous work by Frank Adams.

pendence. Although many worker-owned firms receive professional technical assistance at first, employees gradually take on
more and more responsibility. Employee ownership encourages
people to gain the skills and self-confidence they need to win the
war on poverty.

The largest and most successful example of this approach is
the Workers' Owned Sewing Company in Windsor, North Carolina. Workers' Owned grew out of the ruins of a community-
owned business in 1979. Today the company is a production
cooperative providing steady work at minimum wage for about
fifty members, most of whom are black women. Compared with
the other cases recorded here, the story of Workers' Owned is
perhaps modest, but given the odds against success, it is very
impressive.

The Setting

Bertie County, home of the Workers' Owned Sewing Company, is one of the ten poorest counties in the United States. In
1979 the county's average manufacturing wage was three-fourths
that of the state average, and North Carolina had the lowest
manufacturing wage in the nation. In Bertie County, where most
of the adult males have not completed the eighth grade, unemployment is about 30 percent higher than in any other part of the
state.

In 1980 the *Charlotte News and Observer* described the
county this way:

> The old rhythms of rural life have changed more slowly in
> Bertie County than in most of eastern North Carolina.
> While state planners in high-rise office buildings in Raleigh
> talk about the Sunbelt boom, in Bertie County there is no
> shopping center, no movie theater or even a tractor dealer-
> ship.
>
> While politicians argue the merits of a "New Genera-
> tion" health care plan, a Bertie County mother feeds pow-
> dered Similac to her baby because no one told her the for-

mula should be mixed with water. And while economists call for diversifying the state's economy by bringing in high technology industry, in Bertie County officials are desperate for cut and sew shops to provide jobs for recently displaced sharecroppers.

The dying system of sharecropping has hung on longer, industrial development has come more slowly, and the large landowners have retained more political and economic control than most other places in eastern North Carolina.[1]

Bertie County has never offered much hope for its poor. In recent years a large number of young people have migrated, but for those who have stayed behind few jobs exist. People who are lucky find work at one of the county's peanut-processing plants, tobacco warehouses, sawmills, fish canneries, or, since 1976, Perdue Inc., a chicken-processing plant. For others, there is only seasonal farm work.

Bertie Industries

In 1961 several local black leaders wanted to break through Bertie County's tradition of poverty when they chartered a new company, Bertie Industries. They formed the company not so much to make a profit as to train people for industrial jobs. Bertie Industries raised capital by selling $25 shares to more than 800 county residents. The company bought sewing machines, hired a manager, and put thirty people to work in a cut-and-sew factory as subcontractors to garment manufacturers.

The garment business is unpredictable. Changing seasons and fashions require manufacturers to alter their production, and workers must constantly learn new skills. While this volatility tends to force production costs up, competition between firms creates pressure to hold costs down. Competition is particularly fierce in the South, where there are innumerable small cut-and-sew factories. And since the large manufacturers can pick and choose among these factories for subcontracting work, they can squeeze down prices.

Bertie Industries struggled in this marginal marketplace for a number of years. At one point, when the company was in financial trouble, the community organized the Bertie Booster's Club that, together with the Windsor Merchants' Association, raised $6,000 to pay off the firm's debts. But even this did not keep Bertie Industries from losing a total of $50,000 by 1968. Then in 1969 a federal program saved the company.

The Nixon administration decided to promote a number of companies, including Bertie Industries, as examples of black capitalism. The Small Business Administration (SBA) admitted the company into its Section 8(a) program, which provided defense contracts for minority-owned and economically disadvantaged businesses. Under this program the government offered contracts at rates of 10 to 15 percent above the industry norm.

For a time the company prospered. By 1974 Bertie Industries, with 130 workers, was the sixth-largest employer in the county. The company paid its debts and earned almost $250,000 in profits before taxes. But depending on the Section 8(a) program had its disadvantages. Bertie Industries had come to rely almost exclusively on military contracts and SBA management. The SBA managers, most of whom were white, kept the community board of directors completely uninformed about company operations. Moreover, these managers had no economic incentive to run the company efficiently. When the SBA pulled out of Bertie Industries in 1976 it left the company burdened with a poorly negotiated contract for camouflage jackets. Over the next few years Bertie Industries actually lost $5 on every one of these jackets that it produced.

Soon after the SBA had gone the government canceled a critical defense contract. Within days Bertie Industries closed its doors. Although the company reopened within months, this sequence foreshadowed the pattern of Bertie Industries' troubles for the next three years. Without professional management and favorable contracts the company was plagued with lost orders, payless paydays, and periodic shutdowns. Still carrying the contract for camouflage jackets, Bertie Industries accumulated a debt of $450,000 by 1978. The company shut down again, reopened for a time in 1979, and then closed forever.

Building a Worker-Owned Sewing Company

As a local civil rights activist, Tim Bazemore had been one of the first shareholders of Bertie Industries. In the company's last months he had joined the struggle to keep the production going. After the company closed Bazemore had a new idea. With advice from the Twin Streams Educational Center and the University of North Carolina, Bazemore believed the workers could reopen the cut-and-sew factory as a worker cooperative.

In September 1979 the Workers' Owned Sewing Company was born. Bazemore and three others contributed their time to renovate an old automobile dealership. When they ran out of money Bazemore sold his hogs to pay for the wiring. Then he sold his soybean crop to rent sewing machines and to pay the workers until they had completed some contracts.

Frank Adams, a long-time advocate of employee ownership in North Carolina, spent a year consulting with the Workers' Owned Cooperative, training the workers for democratic self-management. At first Adams had difficulty convincing the workers they should be owners. The workers had become accustomed to the constant crises of Bertie Industries, and many of them had completely lost their investments in that company. "There was no air of euphoria. Unique experiments didn't pay bills. No one knew how long their jobs would last, worker managed or not."[2]

Adams spent his first two weeks working on the production line:

For every dozen garments I tagged I earned eleven cents. For every dozen I bagged I earned another eleven cents. Finally, for every dozen racked for shipment and labeled, I earned yet another eleven cents. If I were to earn $165 a week before taxes, I had to tag, bag, and hang 100 dozen *garments. After watching me for a few minutes, Bazemore said I might reach the goal in three or four years. If I accomplished less, my work would cost the company money."*

Working very hard for low pay characterizes the daily routine for Workers' Owned members. With this same workload Bertie Industries employees had shown very low productivity. Bazemore was gambling that, as owners, the workers would be more productive. During the first week of work, productivity was discouragingly near the Bertie Industries standard. After one month, however, the rate was up 10 percent, and by the end of the year, after completing a long-run contract for boys' pants, the average productivity rate had doubled.

Employee Participation and Employee Attitudes

Although Bazemore owned all the company stock at first, he wanted to introduce participatory management to the workers. The employees elected representatives to the board of directors and the company began holding ten-minute weekly meetings on company and employee time. The company gave up five minutes of production at the end of the day, and workers gave up five minutes by staying late.

Technical experts from Twin Streams and the Industrial Cooperative Association often gave reports to the workers during these meetings. But the workers hardly ever responded. According to Adams,

At no time in their previous working lives had they been expected to talk as an equal to the "boss" or to a business consultant. . . . Throughout most of the meetings the workers sat about in the tiny space set aside for eating. They rarely said a word. Gradually, however, the smaller elected group got acquainted with its role. Opinions were increasingly expressed. Haltingly, they became an assertive force which encouraged fellow workers to clean up the rest rooms, stay longer for weekly meetings with less grouching, and demand more sensitivity from managers.

Nine months after Workers' Owned opened, the worker-elected board took up the issue of whether to require employees to begin buying their $100 shares. Bazemore was against the idea. He was afraid the move would cause some skilled machine operators to quit. Adams reports that Bazemore gave a passionate speech at the board meeting, but

> the silence which followed his lengthy pleas indicated that we'd reached a testing point. Would the six female board members present vote against the founder who also was still the boss? One by one they spoke their minds. No one favored Tim's position. No vote was taken. The sense of the meeting was clear. Tim, to his credit, agreed with his fellow board members, changed his position, and posted the next day the policy requiring payment of the membership fees. By November, 83 percent of the full-time employees had begun buying memberships, and today all fifty full-time members own shares.

The sweltering heat and humidity of eastern North Carolina's summers bore down on Workers' Owned their first year. The cooperative could not afford air conditioning, so the workers voted to move back starting time to five o'clock in the morning. That way they could get in their eight hours before the worst heat of the day.

After a year of operations Workers' Owned had made no substantial profits. But the company had provided steady work; unlike the Bertie Industries experience, there were no shut downs or payless paydays. After he finished his consulting Adams wrote down his impressions of workers' attitudes:

> As one [worker] said, "It's a nicer place to work than some other places, but you don't get no more money with your share." Remuneration, not necessarily self-management or self-acutualization, remained the paramount reason for in-

volvement. Some liked the idea of getting together to talk about and decide on how they'd do work. Others appreciated the fact that no boss stood over them with a stopwatch. On the whole, though, working at Workers' Owned Sewing Company, Inc. was like any other job, and like most business owners the members of Workers' Owned wanted and expected a profit.

As the workers became more interested in improving productivity, they mounted a daily chart to record individual and group accomplishments. They also started taking more pride in their work. Spontaneously they began keeping their machines cleaner and picking up discarded pieces of cloth, and several volunteers cleaned the restroom regularly. Participation also increased. Adams noticed that workers grumbled less at meetings. And while they used to rush away from ten-minute meetings, now workers often stayed for a half hour or more. They even suggested holding weekly potluck lunch meetings, which continue bimonthly today.

Finally, Adams noticed that the board members had become much more knowledgeable about the business. Now they wanted to learn about financing, production methods, personnel policies, and democratic decisionmaking. "In other words, having learned how to run a sewing factory, they wanted to learn how to run it efficiently and democratically."

Bazemore, too, was pleased with the accomplishments of the first year: "We brought the people from a state of limited skills in production to a place where they could excel with a long-run contract. We brought the people from a state of no knowledge of a worker's democracy to a state of some appreciation and general knowledge of a worker-managed production cooperative."

The Cooperative Structure

Workers' Owned has the financial structure of a worker cooperative. Each worker-member has two kinds of equity: stock and an internal capital account. All full-time workers must own one, and only one, share of company stock. When someone new starts at the company he or she has up to six months to begin purchasing a $100 share. Workers can pay for stock through $2 to $5 payroll deductions.

The stock represents a financial commitment of new workers and, since each worker has only one share, the stock also ensures equal voting rights to each member. The managers reserve the right to refuse to sell stock to someone with low productivity. These people cannot become members and must leave the company. According to Bazemore, managers in an industrial cooperative must have the same authority in these situations as their counterparts have in other firms.

In addition to the stock, members have individual internal capital accounts. At the end of each accounting period the cooperative calculates its net earnings (or losses) and then apportions them to workers' capital accounts. Workers' Owned apportions earnings according to workers' total compensation, although other cooperatives divide earnings equally, according to hours worked, by seniority, or by some combination of these methods.

Internal capital accounts do not actually hold cash, although Workers' Owned does plan to pay interest on them. The company makes accounting entries to workers' accounts but reinvests its earnings in new equipment. When worker-members leave the company they must sell back their $100 share of stock and cash in their internal capital account. If the accounts were to build up over a long period of time, they would eventually represent a large liability for the cooperative. To minimize any potential drain on capital, Workers' Owned planned to pay out part of the internal capital accounts to workers as a form of annual profit sharing beginning in 1985.

The cooperative does not pay dividends to workers yet, but it has awarded annual bonuses since 1982. A committee of members sets each worker's bonus based on efficiency level, length of service, tardiness, absenteeism, and voluntary work for the cooperative. Bazemore says that workers have never complained about the fairness of their bonuses. The year-end bonuses averaged about $250 in 1983, $400 in 1984, and $550 in 1985.

Workers' Owned also offers workers productivity incentives on certain contracts. Supervisors set quotas and workers earn a bonus on all work above 80 percent of the quota. On some long-run jobs incentive bonuses help workers raise their earnings from minimum wage to as much as $6 per hour. About three-fourths of the workers receive productivity bonuses, and the company allows employees who cannot raise their productivity at one job to try to earn a bonus at another job.

The company cannot afford health insurance or a pension plan, but the coop does have some fringe benefits. Members may borrow up to $150 interest free from the company for personal expenses. In addition, workers may use part of the company's community garden during the growing season.

Company Performance

Workers' Owned made its first monthly profit eight months after opening, and the number of employees grew from thirty to about fifty-five within a year. But then the company ran into some trouble. In the midst of a nationwide recession the Workers' Owned board faced a tough decision: reduce everyone's hours or lay certain people off. The board decided the company could not afford to lose the production of its most efficient workers, so it laid off workers with the lowest productivity, returning any equity they had in the firm.

By May 1982 the board realized that to achieve long-term stability it needed to change its status in the industry from cut-and-sew subcontracting to direct manufacturing. As a direct manufacturer the cooperative would be able to take a mark-up on raw materials, exert more control over its production scheduling, and receive higher prices by eliminating the middleman.

Before they could aggressively pursue direct contracts, though, the coop members had to improve their capital position; they needed more and better equipment, and they needed cash up front to purchase raw materials. In the next year Workers' Owned raised over $250,000 in grants and loans from churches and foundations and an additional $50,000 from a government job-training program. With this help Bazemore was optimistic that the company would be able to get about 50 percent of its work through direct manufacturing.

The cooperative's first direct contract was from K-Mart and the second, in 1983, was from Sears for 10,000 pairs of jogging shorts. By 1984, 100 percent of Workers' Owned work came from direct contracts. With this new strategy the company's annual sales soared from $600,000 in 1983 to almost $2 million near the end of 1984. That year Workers' Owned built a 5,600-square-foot addition to its plant, rehired the previously laid-off workers, and made plans to hire an additional twenty to thirty workers. The company employed seventy people in early 1986, and Bazemore expected that they would hire another thirty within a year.

Conclusion

Workers' Owned Sewing Company is only six years old, but its early success is promising. The cooperative is not only providing good jobs for people but is giving them pride in ownership and security in future employment—things that traditional enterprises, the community-owned Bertie Industries, and the federal SBA program never ensured. One employee recently summed up her feelings about the cooperative: "You have a job of working for yourself and you're more dedicated to your work and to training new people. We're sort of self-employed and can kick Tim [the manager] around. We really are sold on the idea of working for ourselves . . . we're so determined."

As a microeconomic approach, employee ownership takes advantage of individual self-interest to make workers determined. From his long experience as an activist, Tim Bazemore now believes worker ownership "is the only way low-income people can help themselves in a way that can be permanent." It is to be hoped that Bazemore is right in thinking that where businesses harness the dedication and determination of their workers it may be possible eventually to break the cycle of poverty.

THE LOWE'S COMPANIES: ADAPTING TO GROWTH

Employee-owners of the Lowe's Companies look back at the 1960s and 1970s as an era of remarkable performance. During this period the company grew from a small chain of six hardware stores to the largest retailer of building materials in the United States. In 1961, when the company first shared ownership with its fifty employees, all the Lowe's home centers were clustered in eastern North Carolina. Just twenty years later this retailer of tools, lumber, and electric appliances employed more than 8,000 people in 235 stores across nineteen central and southeastern states. By 1984 the Lowe's Companies reached $1.4 billion in annual sales.

Through all this growth the employees have been sharing in the profits. In 1957 the company began a profit-sharing plan, which invested heavily in Lowe's stock during the 1960s. Lowe's froze the profit-sharing plan in 1978 and established an employee stock ownership plan (ESOP). Today the two plans combined own about 30 percent of the company.

The building materials industry recognizes Lowe's as a leader in motivating workers. The trade journal *Building Supply News* claimed that the company "could publish a textbook on the art of productivity."[1] Bob Strickland, Chairman of Lowe's, agrees. He attributes the firm's phenomenal success to the hard work and determination of the company's employee-owners:

> *How do I know it works? How do I know that Lowe's' growth wasn't influenced more by geography, or the business we're in, or management skill, etc.? In the late*

*'50s and early '60s, there were at least five companies like
ours in the Sunbelt—one in Virginia, one in South Carolina, one in Florida, and two in North Carolina. Same geog-
raphy, same business, different management, of course,
but not bad managements. Three of the companies didn't
make it on their own and sold out. The fourth company is
about one-fourth our size, and they have just adopted an
employee stock ownership plan. Survival of the motivated,
and the productive.[2]*

The Lowe's employee-owners became famous during in the
mid-1970s from reports in the popular press of nonmanagerial
workers who retired from their jobs with enormous amounts of
stock. On August 27, 1971, the *Charlotte Observer* displayed the
front page banner headline: "$125-A-Week Worker Retires
Rich." Ferrell Bryant, a forty-seven-year-old truck driver, retired
after twenty years' work with $413,000 from the profit-sharing
trust. In 1975 *Newsweek* told the story of Charles Valentine, a
warehouse laborer who, like Bryant, earned $125 per week. After
seventeen years working at Lowe's, Valentine retired with stock
worth $666,000. Cecil Murray, personnel manager at Lowe's, left
the company at age fifty with a retirement bundle worth $3.5
million. By 1984 Lowe's had created over fifty employee-owner
millionaires.

The Lowe's success story is all the more impressive because the company has maintained significant employee ownership throughout its rapid growth. Twice in the last two decades
circumstances threatened to diminish or even end employee
ownership at Lowe's. Each time, however, the company adopted
a new strategy, and now Lowe's is one of the largest employee
ownership firms in the country.

Lowe's Early History

Mr. L. S. Lowe opened a hardware store in 1921 in North
Wilkesboro, North Carolina. The store sold notions, snuff, gro-

ceries, hardware, and building materials. Lowe's son, James, and son-in-law, Carl Buchan, operated the business as a partnership in the 1940s, until Buchan bought Lowe out in 1952.

About that time the business took off. Lowe's was a pioneer in the mass marketing of building materials, and the construction boom of the 1950s fueled the company's expansion. Lowe's bought directly from manufacturers and sold directly to contractors and do-if-yourself consumers, thus eliminating the wholesaler's markup and keeping prices down. Indeed, "Lowe's Low Prices" became almost a household phrase in the Southeast.

Lowe's opened its first home center in 1949 in Sparta, North Carolina. Forty miles from the original North Wilkesboro store, the new home center seemed forty years ahead of it in design. The Lowe's home centers were one-stop centers for building materials much as the emerging supermarkets were one-stop centers for grocery shopping. In the next ten years the company added ten more home centers, and sales soared from less than $4 million in 1953 to $27 million in 1959.

Buchan believed this was only the beginning. In 1960 he wrote, "I desire to build this business into the largest and most successful of its type in the world, owned and controlled by those who built it." Buchan intended to sell blocks of his stock periodically to the existing profit-sharing plan during his lifetime and have his estate contribute the balance at his death. But later that year, before he could even begin putting this plan into place, Buchan died at age forty-four.

The management team that Buchan had assembled worked feverishly to salvage the plan for employee ownership. The profit-sharing trust, only three years old, had very limited funds and could not afford to buy the company from Buchan's estate. Early in 1961, however, the managers found a solution. Of the one million extant shares of Lowe's common stock, employees and business associates of Buchan's owned 110,000 shares. The profit-sharing trust bought the remaining 890,000 shares from the Buchan estate for about $6 per share. The trust obtained the cash for this purchase from a short-term loan and then repaid the loan with the proceeds of a public offering of 410,000 shares at

$12.25 per share. Using this strategy employees captured 480,000 shares, or 48 percent, of Lowe's' stock.

Lowe's steady growth of the 1950s accelerated under employee ownership during the next decade. In 1970 the company ran seventy-five stores, sales jumped to $170 million, and Lowe's' net worth had risen from $5 million to $30.5 million. But in one respect this success had become self-defeating: Why should people earning $125 per week keep working when they could retire and collect hundreds of thousands of dollars in stock?

During 1970s Lowe's lost some of its most experienced workers, including five vice-presidents in one year alone. Many of these people were in their late forties or early fifties, and as they retired they took with them millions of dollars in stock from the profit-sharing plan. In 1971 thirteen store managers, salespeople, warehouse workers, and office workers retired and collected a total of $17.5 million.

Also during the 1970s the profit-sharing plan was diversifying its investments. As the company's earlier growth rates began to slow, the plan trustees became concerned about investing so heavily in company stock. Federal law requires that profit-sharing plans and pension plans follow a "prudent man's rule" in making investments. Over the years the amount of profit-sharing plan's assests invested in Lowe's stock ranged between 70 and 90 percent, while other companies generally invested no more than 10 to 25 percent of total profit-sharing funds in their own stock. So in order to maintain "prudence," part of this diversification included a second public offering of stock in 1971, in which Lowe's sold 400,000 shares from the trust.

These two trends—workers retiring with large blocks of stock and the profit-sharing plan diversifying its holdings—were drawing down the amount of stock in the trust. Employee ownership in Lowe's, once almost 50 percent, declined to 17 percent by 1977. Moreover, as the company grew it was forced to divide less and less stock between more and more employees. The result was that the average plan member who had about 5,000 shares in 1968 had only about 1,000 shares in 1975. This dramatic reversal demoralized employees who previously had enjoyed sharing in the growth of their company. The declining employee ownership at Lowe's also seemed to fly in the face of the high acclaim accorded Lowe's by the national media.

Enter the ESOP

In 1977, after reading about legislation making ESOPs a qualified employee benefit plan, Lowe's management announced that it was replacing its almost legendary profit-sharing plan with an employee stock ownership plan. Personnel Manager Ed Spears, recalls the decision to switch to an ESOP:

[The] ESOP gave us an ideal vehicle to continue doing without any feeling of uneasiness what we had been doing all along. The ESOP, even though they had been unfamiliar with it before, looked to our employees to be a lot like our old profit-sharing plan, only less complicated: the same provisions and standards for participation, the same vesting schedule, similar contributions from the company, the same noncontributory status on the part of the employees.[3]

But the new ESOP at Lowe's did provide a number of advantages over the old profit-sharing plan. First, the plan's trustees were free from the fiduciary constraints of diversifying the plan's assets because ESOPs are designed specifically to invest in their companies' stocks. Second, Lowe's could contribute up to 25 percent of covered payroll to the ESOP and still qualify for a tax deduction. Under the profit-sharing plan Lowe's could make contributions only out of its profits, but with the ESOP it could make contributions regardless of corporate profit. Finally, under the ESOP Lowe's could either contribute cash to buy outstanding shares or contribute newly issued shares. By contributing new shares to the ESOP Lowe's could claim a cash tax deduction for a noncash expense.

When making the change to the ESOP Lowe's froze the assets of the profit-sharing plan and fully vested all profit-sharing participants, regardless of their length of service. In order to make the changeover as beneficial as possible, Lowe's gave employees a choice of one of ten ways to freeze their profit-sharing accounts, starting with 100 percent cash, then 90 percent cash and 10 percent stock, and so on down to 10 percent cash and 90 percent stock.

The response was overwhelming: 79 percent of Lowe's employees requested the 90 percent stock, 10 percent cash split, and another 11 percent chose 80 percent stock, 20 percent cash. The employee requests amounted to 2.7 million shares, but at the time the trust had only 2.2 million shares of Lowe's stock. In effect the employees were saying that there was not enough stock in the plan to satisfy them. According to a Lowe's annual report this was "a real testimonial to their desire for Lowe's stock, and to the decision to switch to the new Employee Stock Ownership Plan."[4] As of January 1, 1978, the company fixed the amount of cash and stock in each participant's profit-sharing account. In the future when workers retired, they would receive the entire amount of their frozen profit-sharing accounts plus any accumulated dividends and income.

All full-time employees are eligible to participate in the Lowe's ESOP after ninety days. Employees become fully vested in the plan after fifteen years. Vesting begins after the second year at 10 percent and builds at 5 percent per year, reaching 50 percent after ten years. From the eleventh through the fifteenth years vesting continues at 10 percent per year. Lowe's allocates shares to employees according to salary.

Because Lowe's is a publicly traded company, workers can vote their allocated shares. Management has found the voting rights pass through to be a distinct advantage. "The fact of the matter is," says Washington attorney and ESOP advocate Norman Kurland, "the employees at Lowe's have been vastly more supportive of management's position than the outside shareholders. The employees know what is going on, and, to the extent that management's position is sound, the employee vote is never a problem. In fact, it is a boon."[5]

Of the seven members of Lowe's' board of directors, six are founding members, having served since Carl Buchan appointed them years ago. Four board members are Lowe's employees, although no nonmanagerial employees serve on the board. As current board members retire the stockholders will choose their replacements.

Although Lowe's has no formal participation programs, each home center does have weekly employee meetings. Employees in each store also elect one representative to the companywide ESOP advisory committee, which meets periodically to hear management reports and formulate recommendations to management. Former advisory committee president, David Sain, described the committee as "a total involvement-type program that has definitely made a difference among all our employees."[6]

Communicating the idea of ownership to employees in a company as large and spread out as Lowe's could be a problem. But company president Bob Strickland believes Lowe's handles it effectively, and in a recent survey 75 percent of the employees responding said that they have a clear understanding of the ESOP. In each store the elected representatives bring back information and written documents from ESOP advisory committee meetings. Lowe's has produced a videotape on the ESOP for employees, complete with scenes from Wall Street and an interview with ESOP originator Louis Kelso. Employees also receive Lowe's award-winning annual reports, noted for their clear and easy-to-read descriptions of company operations.

Employee Attitudes

Bob Strickland is convinced that employee ownership is the key to success at Lowe's. On more than one occasion he has traveled to Washington to testify before Congress. He speaks powerfully about his beliefs:

Reindustrializing this country is a must. But as we get on with the job, we need to keep a few things in mind. While reindustrializing with new plants and equipment, we also

*need to be revitalizing the attitude and motivation of the
workers. . . . I'm convinced that a proven way to revitalize
the motivation of our workers is to give them a piece of the
action through employee stock ownership. Lowe's' people
believe in employee stock ownership. We believe it is creative capitalism and are more firmly committed to the
concept than ever before.[7]*

A manager at one of the company's home centers agrees
that the ESOP has been crucial in motivating workers: "I have
never known of another company where the desires of the employees are as closely tied to those of top management. Everyone
here has a common concern: the bottom line."

In 1983 the National Center for Employee Ownership
(NCEO) surveyed a random 7 percent sample of Lowe's employees and found that, in general, the workers, too, believe employee ownership is part of the reason Lowe's is so successful.
Almost three-fifths of the respondents said that they work harder
because of their ownership. Well over 80 percent of the employees responded that they were proud to own stock in the
company, that the ESOP was important to them, and that owning stock made them more interested in Lowe's' financial performance.[8]

The study found that employees who are higher paid and
who have been with the company longer are particularly satisfied with Lowe's. They scored higher than lower paid and shorter
term employees on measures of organizational commitment, pay
satisfaction, and satisfaction with the ESOP. This result may in
part reflect the relatively long vesting schedule at Lowe's. As one
worker puts it in the survey: "At this time, with five years invested in this company, I would be given only 25 percent of $26,-
400, or $6,000. That's not enough of an influence over me to
worry about ESOP or company policies, so that I work harder,
nor does it give me enough influence to enter into corporate
policy or procedure matters."

This employee was not alone in expressing a desire to participate more in company decisionmaking. In a company where

employees are so enthusiastic about the employee ownership plan, the respondents were unusually dissatisfied with their degree of influence. Almost half the employees indicated that they have little or no say over how they do their own jobs, and close to 90 percent responded that they have no say or only receive information about corporate policy. Again, this may be due to the relatively long vesting period. Also, although employees do have full voting rights, they have not yet had an opportunity to elect members of the board.

The Future

Louis Kelso once called the Lowe's profit-sharing plan the most successful example of what employee ownership might achieve. It is true that Lowe's has demonstrated an uncommon ability to share wealth with both its employees and its outside investors. And now, with the increasing numbers of do-it-yourself builders and the shift in population and business growth to the sunbelt, the future of Lowe's continues to look prosperous.

In 1960 Lowe's set out to build the largest company in the retail hardware business. It succeeded. In 1971 Lowe's said it would reach $1 billion in sales volume in a decade. It did. Today Bob Strickland discusses the future in terms of one-year plans, five-year goals, and ten-year dreams. Strickland compares Lowe's market share, just 2 percent, with market shares of other firms that are leaders in their industries, and he plans Lowe's future success.

What about the future of employee ownership at Lowe's? Employee ownership almost failed to get off the ground because of Carl Buchan's untimely death. Later, the company's very success undermined the employees' profit-sharing plan as employees cashed in their valuable accounts. But today Buchan's dream that Lowe's would be owned and controlled by those who have built it has, at least partly, come true. Employee ownership is growing again. In 1983 the ESOP held 15 percent of Lowe's stock, worth over $100 million. The frozen profit-sharing plan held another 15 percent. Each year Lowe's contributes between

12 and 15 percent of company payroll to the ESOP, amounting to 500,000 new shares in 1982.

In 1978 U.S. Senator Mike Gravel (D-AL) asked Bob Strickland during a Finance Committee hearing if Lowe's had a target for its percentage of employee stock ownership. Strickland told the senator that a fifty-fifty mix seemed appropriate. A year later Strickland had another opportunity to speak to Gravel: "I told him that I had thought many times about his question, and with hindsight, I'd changed my goal. I don't want our employees to own 50 percent—I want them to own at least 51 percent!"[9]

14

ONCE AGAIN NUT BUTTER, THE COMMON GROUND, AND FREEWHEEL BICYCLE: WORKER COOPERATIVES AND DEMOCRATIC DECISIONMAKING

Worker ownership and workplace democracy are related, but not necessarily convergent, phenomena. As the case studies in this volume show, companies with employee ownership plans share management of the firm with employees to varying degrees. Many employee stock ownership plans (ESOP), for example, do not pass through voting rights and have only limited participation programs; other employee ownership companies, including a number of ESOPs, are much more democratic, with stock voting rights, workers on the board of directors, and workers participating in shopfloor decisionmaking.

Of all the types of employee ownership, worker cooperatives most commonly organize democratic workplaces. In this respect the chief distinction between cooperatives and other employee-owned corporations is the distribution of voting rights. Voting rights in cooperatives are personal rights based on membership, not property rights based on stock ownership, as in ESOPs, for example. Thus, workers have the right to share equally in the governance of a cooperative. This principle of one person, one vote is fundamental to both workplace democracy and worker cooperatives; yet, simple as the principle sounds, different cooperatives practice it in different ways, as the following examples demonstrate.

Once Again Nut Butter

Perhaps one of the most common images of workplace democracy is that of all workers participating in all decisions, or at least in all important decisions. While this would bring chaos to a company the size of General Motors, many small worker cooperatives do make decisions collectively.

Jeremy Thayler is one of five members of the Once Again Nut Butter Collective in Nunda, New York. The Once Again collective manufacturers peanut butter, mostly for distribution to consumer cooperatives in the Northeast. Thayler describes the collective as "an experiment in consensus" where each member has an equal say in decisions. But the group tries not to bring issues to a vote, preferring to settle them by mutual agreement.

Once Again Nut Butter has no formal management structure. Members perform several tasks and rotate jobs periodically, some jobs weekly, others monthly or yearly, some even over a multiyear period, depending on how dull the jobs are or what skills workers need to complete them. In the same day a collective member might work on the front office staff and then run a peanut-butter–making machine. Thayler was the company's buyer for three years, ordering everything from peanuts and jars to expensive new equipment. That job required special skills, but Thayler believes that with a little training and encouragement "everyone can do it."

Throughout the early 1980s the collective was going strong, selling $700,000 worth of peanut butter in 1983 alone and clearing $40,000 in profits. Because of its success Once Again Nut Butter is able to pay its workers fairly well. All members receive the identical wage of $8 per hour, complete medical benefits, and a weekly family support bonus of seven hours pay per child.

The collective is careful with its resources and actively reinvests in new machinery. In fact, as Once Again Nut Butter

140

has grown it has become quite capital intensive. Relying on new equipment instead of new labor helps to maximize returns per worker; it also allows the collective to keep its number of members low. A small membership is essential to consensual decisionmaking, and management by consensus is a priority for the Once Again collective members.

The Once Again Nut Butter Collective provides one of the most democratic workplaces imaginable. But consensus is difficult to maintain in groups much larger than Once Again's five members and seriously breaks down in groups of ten or more. Larger worker cooperatives, therefore, have organized other means for institutionalizing workplace democracy.

The Common Ground

On the second floor of an old firehouse in Brattleboro, Vermont, the Common Ground Restaurant offers its patrons a menu of all-natural foods. Originally an investor-owned corporation, the Common Ground was started in 1971 by a group of 200 Brattleboro-area residents. They were looking for a place to eat natural food in an atmosphere appealing to their "vegetarian and philosophical tastebuds."[1]

Over a period of years several hired managers burned themselves out working at the Common Ground, and in 1977 the shareholders decided to sell to the employees. The new worker-owners restructured the business as a worker cooperative, which by 1984 had thirteen full-time members and about ten part-time nonmembers.

It is important to the members of the Common Ground to work in an environment consistent with their values, so the restaurant has maintained its original character since becoming a coop. According to one member the Common Ground caters to a "politically aware clientele," and in many ways it is reminiscent of the 1960s. In 1983, for example, the restaurant added a two-cent surcharge to a cup of coffee and split the proceeds—about $100 per month—between medical aid for El Salvador and a Guatemalan refugee group. The coop also lets community groups use its space for meetings, and at Thanksgiving the Common Ground sponsors a free community dinner for 150 people—the "high point of the year."

Common Ground has established certain criteria for workers to meet in order to become members. First, potential members must demonstrate, through discussions and work, that they are committed to the values of the cooperative. Then the membership votes on admission, a two-thirds majority being needed for acceptance. New members must pay a $5 membership fee and purchase a share of stock for $200. All workers share profits and tips equally, and the ratio of the highest to the lowest salary is 1.3 to 1.

The Common Ground has no board of directors and no hierarchy of management levels. After taking over from the shareholders the members attempted to manage the restaurant by consensus, but this system developed serious problems. Waiting for all members to reach agreement paralyzed the decisionmaking process and began hurting the cooperative's finances. In addition, the consensual arrangement had no mechanism for task accountability, and some workers felt they were doing more than their share of work.

In 1981 the Common Ground created a policymaking committee to bring order into its management. All worker-members have the opportunity to be on this committee on a rotating basis. The policy committee, which meets every three weeks, acts as a forum for worker comments and ideas and has decisionmaking authority on general issues. The Common Ground also has about a dozen area-specific committees on which both members and nonmembers serve. These include the financial committee and committees for hiring, grievance, scheduling, maintenance, menu and pricing, music, long-range planning, and advertising and public relations. The entire staff, members and nonmembers, meets once a month and may overturn committee decisions by a two-thirds vote, except for financial and long-range planning decisions, over which only members have final authority.

Individual workers still make decisions about how to do a

particular job. They also rotate jobs, but not on any prescribed basis, and anyone with the interest and initiative can take reponsibility for a new area. For example, Bari Madwin managed the expansion of the Common Ground catering service, an outgrowth of the restaurant. Kevin Connors oversaw the production of a new Common Ground dessert cookbook, and several other members pitched in with calligraphy and artwork.

Members of the Common Ground cooperative are extraordinarily satisfied according to the National Center for Employee Ownership (NCEO) survey results.[2] In fact, their scores on measures of job satisfaction, organizational commitment, work motivation, and job effort were among the highest the NCEO has recorded. The only area in which respondents were somewhat less satisfied was with their pay, which ranges from $3.50 per hour for part-time nonmembers to $5.00 per hour for full-time members. But workers realize that low pay is the price of participating in an alternative foods restaurant. As one member put it, "That is a trade-off made to be in control of our work life. It is a conscious decision and a worthwhile one to us."

Kevin Connors, a six-year Common Ground veteran, believes that "working democratically doesn't mean everyone is involved in every decision." And Common Ground, with its committee system, has moved away from decisionmaking by consensus and taken one step toward a more representative workplace democracy. The Common Ground is a liberal variety of representative democracy, though, since every member may choose to sit on the policy committee and workers maintain significant job autonomy. The Common Ground is midway between worker cooperatives run by consensus, such as Once Again Nut Butter, and coops with more structured management, such as Freewheel Bicycle.

Freewheel Bicycle

Eight Minnesotan cyclists started the Minneapolis Freewheel Bicycle cooperative in 1974. Undercapitalized at first, the coop opened with a small inventory of bicycles and biking accessories. Selling mostly to university students, Freewheel's sales increased every year from under $50,000 in 1975 to $870,000 by 1982. As the coop grew it expanded its bicycle line and added cross-country ski, camping, and exercise equipment. Freewheel outgrew its original space and moved to a new and larger store in 1982.

Freewheel now has thirteen full-time members and hires twenty to thirty part-time seasonal workers. A member must first work 1,200 hours as a nonmember and then receive a majority acceptance vote of members. New members must pay a one-time $10 fee, buy stock over a four-year period through a 5 percent payroll deduction, and attend at least two membership meetings per year.

Freewheel pays members and nonmembers according to the same scale. Managers receive the highest salary, but new workers with no skills earn 70 percent as much as managers, and their wages increase by 5 percent annually. Members of the cooperative, of course, have the advantage of owning the assets of the firm and sharing in its profits. Each year Freewheel calculates its after-tax earnings and decides what percentage of these to distribute to members and what percentage to reinvest. In the late 1970s and early 1980s Freewheel was distributing between 25 and 50 percent of earnings to members in cash payments. In one year this amounted to an average of $2,750 for each member. The cooperative reinvests the remaining earnings, crediting them to members' internal accounts that provide a source of interest-free financing for Freewheel while members stay with the company. When members leave Freewheel, or if they ever decide to liquidate the company, they receive the value of their internal accounts.

Like the members of the Common Ground and other young idealists who start cooperatives, Freewheel's members tried to manage the bicycle shop by consensus for several years. But as the business grew and the membership changed this system became so cumbersome that by 1981 the group decided to overhaul its management structure. Freewheel developed three reporting levels of management: the board of directors, supervisors, and everyone else.

The six members of the Freewheel board of directors meet every two weeks. Employees elect board members to fill specific vacancies, such as financial officer or one of the supervisory positions. All employees may attend board meetings, and each quarter the cooperative holds a general meeting in which everyone may participate.

Freewheel has two formal worker participation groups, one for salespeople and the other for workers in the repair shop. These groups discuss productivity, timeliness, new products, sales, and "almost everything dealing with the operation of the cooperative." If a group can't settle a controversial matter, the board of directors decides.

The employees at Freewheel are quite happy with their jobs, though not as enthusiastic as members of the Common Ground, according to NCEO's 1984 survey. Some employee responses suggest that Freewheel has had difficulty striking a balance between its earlier collective decisionmaking and some of the more traditional management styles it has recently adopted. But Freewheel is similar to a number of worker cooperatives that have constructed democratic workplaces where elected representatives, not the workers themselves, manage the firm.

The Forms of Workplace Democracy

If workplace democracy comes in a variety of flavors, then worker cooperatives have the richest ingredients. Cooperatives attract members for whom control over their work is a lifetime goal. The three examples in this chapter are not exhaustive of the possibilities for democratic cooperatives, but they do illustrate a variety of cooperative governance structures, from the ultrademocratic decisionmaking at Once Again Nut Butter to the more republican (with a small r) system at Freewheel Bicycle.

The experiences of Once Again, Common Ground, and

Freewheel support at least one conclusion: The larger a cooperative becomes the less everyone can participate in making decisions. Worker cooperatives in France, Italy, Israel, and the Mondragon region of Spain have learned this same lesson. The large industrial cooperatives of Europe have developed sophisticated mechanisms to ensure the participation rights of individual workers while maintaining efficient decisionmaking.

Democratic management and efficient management are not incongruous concepts, but rather self-reinforcing if combined in the right balance. As a larger and more industrial cooperative sector emerges in the United States, cooperatives will have to develop professional managerial and technical expertise. In the last five years this has already begun with groups like the Somerville, Massachusetts-based Industrial Cooperative Association, which provides technical assistance to democratic, worker-owned businesses. Such developments are encouraging since they point toward a future where large democratic workplaces will compete successfully in our national economy.

EPILOGUE: THE FUTURE OF EMPLOYEE OWNERSHIP

Now that we have examined the current national trends in employee ownership and participation, the inner workings of employee ownership, and a selection of notable examples, let's consider where all of this is going.

Employee ownership will probably come to play a much larger role in the economy. If the number of workers in employee ownership companies continues to grow as fast as it has in the last decade, it is likely that ten to twenty percent of the nongovernment workforce will work for companies that are at least 15 percent employee owned within the next thirty to fifty years. This development would no doubt change the way unions, business, and the public perceive and respond to employee ownership.

Unions

Trade unions now represent about 15 percent of the private sector workforce, a figure that could decline to as low as 10 percent according to some labor economists. To date they have played a relatively passive role in employee ownership. But if employee ownership continues to grow, it will be hard for unions not to become more actively involved.

Unions could take a new approach toward employee ownership, for instance, by identifying all current unionized employee ownership firms and providing them with customized services. Such firms might even constitute a special Employee Ownership

Sector in the trade union movement such as the Hevrat Ovdim of Israel's General Federation of Labor. In nonunionized companies unions could represent the interests of employee-owners and provide them with useful services through some form of associate membership. In companies where workers feel their rights have been abused or their desire for involvement unfulfilled, unions could mount full-fledged organization campaigns.

Unions might use a small percentage of their pension funds and their technical expertise to help their unemployed and under-employed members start worker-owned, unionized companies. They could also become more involved in structuring deals that are more representative of the interests of their members.

While employee ownership raises a number of important questions about how a union can and should function in a worker-owned firm, there is little benefit for unions or their members in simply avoiding the issue.

On a more general level, some believe that the difference between labor and capital will be eliminated by a new type of company. It is true that labor is employing capital more and that capital is viewing workers as much more than a mere production cost. Workers are now sources of equity under a variety of alternatives in stock ownership, pension plans, wage flexibility, and group incentive plans. Can these changes be perceived as a new form of labor-management cooperation, or are they just new tools in the same old struggle?

Business

Just as employee ownership presents both challenges and opportunities to unions, so it does to business. As the cases in this book have shown, employee ownership can be a way to motivate employees, cut waste, generate new ideas, save taxes, and reward workers in a way that shares growth rather than depletes cash flow. Employee ownership may grow simply because employee ownership companies out-compete conventionally owned firms. Yet, if poorly managed, employee ownership can be little more than an inconsequential benefit or, worse, can actually cause employee cynicism and disaffection.

For most managers the first question will always be, Do we really want to share ownership? No matter how quickly employee ownership grows, or how impressive its financial planning benefits might become, there will always be those who believe that the traditional separation between capital-providing owners and hired laborers is more sensible, fair, and practical.

For those who do accept the idea of shared ownership, the next question will be how to manage when workers are owners. How much power can and should be ceded? How far should companies go in reorganizing jobs? What percentage of the company should employees own?

Predicting how far employee ownership will go in penetrating management reluctance to share ownership and reform work is hazardous conjecture. But the growth and performance of employee ownership over the last decade makes it clear that the idea can no longer be ignored. Many employee ownership companies have become industry leaders. Many banks, lawyers, accountants, and consultants have a vested stake in promoting employee ownership. Many federal and state laws encourage it. But all of this does not yet guarantee that employee ownership will become a significant factor in reinventing the corporation.

The Public

Finally, citizens, researchers, and government policymakers will continue to debate whether and how our laws, particularly the tax system, should be structured to encourage employee ownership and other forms of increased worker involvement. Most people are genuinely attracted to the idea of broadened ownership and view it as a sensible approach to bringing democratic values and goals into the economy. A Peter Hart poll in the 1970s found that most Americans would prefer to work for employee ownership companies. This support is reflected in broad political support, which should survive Senator Russell Long's departure from Congress at the end of 1986.

149

But how will the idea stand up to attempts to cut the budget deficit by cutting tax incentives? Will the public continue to support employee ownership even as its cost grows? It appears the answer is yes. Given an opportunity to cut basic ESOP incentives in both 1984 and 1986, Congress chose to preserve them and in 1984 even expanded them in a bill designed to cut the deficit. The most expensive (and least important) part of ESOP law, the "tax credit ESOPs," will expire at the end of 1987 or earlier, to the regret of few.[1] In the future, sizably and majority employee-owned firms will probably play a more central role in the public imagination because of the reduced tax incentives for these tax credit plans.

Given the attention employee ownership companies have received for their propensity to experiment with labor-management cooperation, work innovation, wage flexibility, and other important concepts, the tax incentives are, in effect, buying an American experiment to transform work and the corporation. This is not only defensible, but desirable as we confront the challenges of a competitive world economy.

In addition, legislative support at the state and local levels should also continue to grow, especially for worker buyouts. Since the first state law in 1979, half of the U.S. population has become covered by such state legislation. Worker buyouts of failing firms and concession bargaining for ownership plans in hard-pressed industries such as steel, trucking, and airlines generally cost the taxpayer nothing, since these companies do not pay taxes if they are not profitable.[2]

As one labor leader comments, distress buyouts "can be defensible as adjustment mechanisms to help people deal with the transformation of the economy. These are desparate times in some industries and employee ownership helps us buy time and keep jobs available."[3] Some of these cases may be turned into successes through serious reorganization of companies. Others will allow workers to preserve their jobs through their own sacrifices. Either way, continuing employment will save taxpayers massive costs in unemployment compensation, welfare benefits, the loss of federal and state income and other taxes, and the effects of the increased pressure on government services as a result of personal and economic dislocation.[4]

Emerging Issues in Employee Ownership

The growth of employee ownership will raise many important issues—issues that will require resolution if the idea is to achieve its potential. For instance, employees, unions, managers, and the government will have to look at worker rights from a somewhat different perspective. National labor law was written when workers worked and managers managed. As growing numbers of employees own companies and participate in management, and as managers and entrepreneurs work with employees in increasingly flexible and cooperative companies, a new form of labor-business organization may evolve.

Business Week discussed these problems in a cover story and an article on labor law, noting that "many provisions of U.S. law could actually hinder cooperative efforts to raise productivity and improve quality."[5] Scholars are now debating what the basic rights of workers in largely employee-owned businesses should be,[6] and the U.S. Department of Labor has initiated a two-year study to explore conflicts between federal law and various forms of worker participation.

A number of issues are raised here. First, there is the issue of what rights, if any, the federal government should ensure worker-owners. Take an extreme example: An ESOP was set up by a group of managers who controlled the company's board, appointed the ESOP trustee, and gave employees nonvoting shares. Except for a sign that read "Owners' Washroom," little changed at the company. Subsequently, management decided to sell the company to another firm without consulting the workers.[7] Although federal legislation has since made the sale of an ESOP company a mandatory issue for employee voting, this case does raise important questions. Should workers be guaranteed a larger role? If they are, would fewer companies set up employee ownership plans? Are workers better off with an ESOP and no control than with no ESOP at all? What should be the tradeoff between encouraging employee ownership and protecting workers?

On the other hand, what happens when a union actively promotes employee control or takes seats on the board? Is this, or should it be, a violation of the National Labor Relations Act prohibitions against unions bargaining with themselves?

Another intriguing issue is how employee ownership will help us deal with economic change. Large sectors of employee ownership firms in the economy could perhaps be a stabilizing influence, if, as some believe, the need for workers declines in the United States. Many small highly automated businesses, for instance, have radically eliminated the need for labor as a factor in production in favor of capital and knowledge. At the same time, capital has become increasingly mobile, with entire factories moving overseas and some large companies only maintaining U.S. headquarters as they shift increasing amounts of their job-creating work abroad.

If labor-intensive service industries cannot absorb or provide a decent standard of living for unemployed, underemployed, or new workers, then people will need additional sources of income as employment is reduced and capital-intensive businesses expand. If a small number of people own most of the capital, they alone will benefit from technological advances while those with no capital holdings are forced into a condition of dependence.

By contrast, employee ownership companies have an incentive to find ways of managing economic change while remembering their commitment to job creation. Employee ownership companies could respond to change by reducing hours, not laying off workers, or providing early retirement. In either case, the capital stake of workers could compensate for their loss of labor income.

More speculatively, if more companies were employee owned, and were joined in mutual-aid associations with their own banks and technical assistance departments, then changes in markets, fluctuations in demand, and the need to reduce employment or change products might not create such havoc.

Workers could move more easily from declining to emerging industries, or even start their own new companies.

Indeed, two highly successful versions of this scenario now exist in other countries. There are over 100,000 people in Israel's *kibbutzim* with hundreds of industries divided into three conglomerate-type mutual-aid federations.[8] Also there is the 20,000-worker Mondragon federation of cooperatives in the Basque region of Spain, which has proven quite adept at managing economic fluctuations.[9] Both organizations have highly productive export-oriented capital-intensive industries and neither accepts government transfer payments. They manage to increase their dependence on technology instead of labor, avoid unemployment, and develop new businesses at the same time by careful planning and continual retraining and education. These examples suggest the possibility of a private sector alternative to government planning for economic dislocations.

A Culture of Employee Ownership

Will employee ownership be just another benefit plan or merely a means to improve productivity, or will it become rooted in the expectations of workers and the cultures of corporations? Much attention—and much envy—has been awarded to Japan's successful corporate culture. But while Americans can import Japanese products, they cannot import Japanese culture and personality. Any substantive reform of the corporation in this country must have a decidedly American flavor and cultural base or it will not spread. It must stress elements all Americans share yet be adaptive enough to attract subgroups as profoundly different as ethnics in Somerville, Massachusetts, young professionals in Vienna, Virginia, low-income blacks in Windsor, North Carolina, and sixties idealists in California. We believe employee ownership can provide these common elements. Ownership is a basic American value deeply held by many people. It may well form the basis for lasting and important corporate change.

It would be mere speculation to guess whether employee

ownership will in fact be the catalyst for a new American company—one that provides more participation and responsibility and shares short- and long-term corporate growth with employees. The companies profiled here vary in how closely they approach this idealized notion, but they all stimulate our sense of possibility.

Presenting snapshots of a wide array of employee ownership companies, this book takes stock of employee ownership in the United States. Perhaps most important, the cases show the flexibility of employee ownership and the diversity of companies with employee ownership plans. Most of the companies are not dramatic or glamorous. They are, overall, profitable firms that have set up their plans for a variety of reasons. They are companies both large and small, public and private, with and without unions, and in every kind of industry. But generally they do have in common a belief that employee ownership is a good idea and a dedication that makes that idea work—both for the company and the employees.

While typical in that they represent broadly the employee ownership landscape, most of these companies are unusually successful with their employee ownership programs. Many have created workplaces that are genuinely more satisfying, employees who are often more motivated and committed, and corporate performance that is generally above average or exceptional. In addition to all this, and certainly most striking, they are affecting a transfer of wealth potentially more significant than anything since the Homestead Act. Without question these companies provide working models for the corporate America of the future—models we all need to examine as we approach the twenty-first century.

NOTES

Preface

1. "Workstyle: A Whole New Way to Manage Your People," *Inc.* (February 1986): 45.
2. *People and Productivity: A Challenge to Corporate America* (New York: New York Stock Exchange, Office of Economic Research, 1982), p. 44.
3. Robert H. Guest, *Innovative Work Practices*, Work in America Institute Studies in Productivity, Number 21 (New York: Pergamon, 1982).

Chapter 1

1. Corcy Rosen, Katherine Klein, and Karen Young, *Employee Ownership in America: The Equity Solution* (Lexington, Mass.: Lexington Books, 1986), p. 263.
2. U.S. Congress, Joint Economic Committee, *Broadening the Ownership of New Capital: ESOPs and Other Alternatives*, Joint Committee Print, 94th Cong., 2d sess., 1976.
3. Richard Patard, "Employee Ownership in the 1920's," 1982. (Unpublished.)
4. Louis Kelso and Patricia Hetter, *Two-Factor Theory: The Economics of Reality* (New York: Vintage, 1967).
5. Michael Conte and Arnold Tannenbaum, *Employee Ownership* (Ann Arbor: University of Michigan Survey Research Center, 1980).
6. Thomas Marsh and Dale McAllister, "ESOP's Tables," *Journal of Corporation Law*, no. 3 (Spring 1981): 613–17.
7. Katherine Klein and Corey Rosen, "Job Generation Performance of Employee Owned Companies," *Monthly Labor Review* 106, no. 8 (August 1983): 15–19.

8. Ira Wagner, "Employee Ownership in Corporate America," Report to the New York Stock Exchange (Arlington, Va.: National Center for Employee Ownership, 1984).

9. Richard Cavanaugh, *The Winning Performance of America's Mid-Sized Companies* (Chicago: McKenzie, 1983).

10. Arnold Tannenbaum, Harold Cook, and Jack Lohman, *The Relationship of Employee Ownership to the Technological Apartiveness and Performance of Companies* (Ann Arbor: University of Michigan Institute for Social Research, 1984).

11. Klein and Rosen, "Job Generation Performance of Employee Owned Companies."

12. U.S. General Accounting Office, "Initial Results of a Survey on Employee Stock Ownership Plans" (Washington, D.C.: GAO/PEMD–85–11, 1985).

13. Corey Rosen and Jonathan Feldman, "Employee Benefits in Employee Stock Ownership Plans," *Pension World* 22, no. 2 (February 1986): 34–39.

14. Klein and Rosen, "Job Generation Performance of Employee Owned Companies."

15. Katrina Berman, "The Worker Owned Plywood Companies," in Joyce Rothschild-Whitt and Frank Lindenfeld, eds., *Workplace Democracy and Social Change* (Boston, Mass.: Porter-Sargent, 1982), pp. 161–76.

16. Rosen, Klein, and Young, *Employee Ownership in America.*

Chapter 2

1. This and all ensuing quotes are from National Center for Employee Ownership, *M. W. Carr Case Study and Interviews* (Arlington, Va.: NCEO, 1982).

Chapter 3

1. This and all ensuing quotes are from National Center for Employee Ownership, *Evaluation Research Corporation Case Study and Interviews* (Arlington, Va.: NCEO, 1982).

2. Corey Rosen, Katherine Klein, and Karen Young, *Employee Ownership in America: The Equity Solution* (Lexington, Mass.: Lexington Books, 1986).

Chapter 4

1. Quad/Graphics, Inc., *Quad/Graphics Annual Report: 1983* (Pewaukee, Wis.: Quad/Graphics, 1984), p. 1.

2. Ellen Wojahn, "Management By Walking Away," *Inc.* (October 1983): 72.

3. Ibid.

4. Quad/Graphics, *Annual Report: 1983*, p. 25.

5. Wojahn, "Management By Walking Away," p. 70.

6. Ibid.

7. Quad/Graphics, *Quad/Graphics Annual Report: 1983*.

8. National Center for Employee Ownership, *Quad/Graphics Case Study and Interviews* (Arlington, Va.: NCEO, 1984).

Chapter 5

1. Veljoko Rus, "Yugoslav Self-Management—30 Years Later," in Bernhard Wilpert and Arnot Surge, ed., *International Perspectives on Organizational Democracy* (New York: Wiley, 1984); Vlado Arzensek, "Problems in Yugoslav Self-Management, " in Colin Crouch and Frank A. Heller, eds., *Organizational Democracy and Political Processes* (New York: Wiley, 1983).

2. National Center for Employee Ownership, *Phillips Paper Corporation Case Study and Interviews* (Arlington, Va.: NCEO, 1983).

3. Ibid.

Chapter 6

1. This and all ensuing quotes are from National Center for Employee Ownership, *Hyatt-Clark Industries Case Studies and Interviews* (Arlington, Va.: NCEO, 1983).

2. Ibid.

Chapter 8

1. This and all ensuing quotes are from National Center for Employee Ownership, *Allied Plywood Case Study and Interviews* (Arlington, Va.: NCEO, 1982).

2. Ibid.

Chapter 9

1. This and all ensuing quotes are from National Center for Employee Ownership, *Fastener Industries Case Studies and Interviews* (Arlington, Va.: NCEO, 1983).

2. Corey Rosen, Katherine Klein, and Karen Young, *Employee Ownership in America: The Equity Solution* (Lexington, Mass.: Lexington Books, 1986).

3. National Center for Employee Ownership, *Fastener Industries Case Studies.*

Chapter 10

1. Wallace Johnson, *A Fresh Look at Patriotism: New Directions for America* (Old Greenwich, Conn.: Devin-Adair, 1976).

2. Up-Right, Inc., "Up-Right Employee Stock Ownership Plan Handbook" (Berkeley: ESOP Association of America, 1975).

3. National Center for Employee Ownership, *Up-Right, Inc. Case Study and Interviews* (Arlington, Va.: NCEO, 1983).

Chapter 11

1. For a review of these see Deborah Groban Olson, "Union Experience with Worker Ownership," *Wisconsin Law Review* 5 (1982).

Chapter 12

1. " 'Changes' Come Slowly for Poor, Rural Bertie," *Charlotte News & Observer*, January 7, 1980.

2. This and all ensuing quotes are from Frank Adams, *Making Production, Making Democracy: A Case Study of Teaching in the Workplace* (Chapel Hill, N.C.: Twin Streams Educational Center, 1982).

Chapter 13

1. Lowe's Is Shooting for a Bigger League," *Building Supply News* (January 1983).

2. Robert Strickland, "Testimony to the United States Senate Committee on Finance," May 19, 1981.

3. National Center for Employee Ownership, *The Lowe's Companies Case Study and Interviews* (Arlington, Va.: NCEO, 1983).

4. Lowe's Company, *Annual Report: 1977* (North Wilkesboro, N.C.: Lowe's Co., 1978).

5. Norman Kurland, Panel Presentation at the First Annual Employee Ownership and Participation Conference, Boston, Mass., April 1982.

158

6. ESOP Association of America, "The Lowe's Companies ESOP" (Berkeley: ESOP Association of America, no date).

7. Robert Strickland, "The Lowe's ESOP," Presentation at the Second Annual ESOP Symposium, Georgetown University Law School, Washington, D.C., September 15, 1980.

8. National Center for Employee Ownership, *The Lowe's Companies Case Study;* ESOP Association, "The Lowe's Companies ESOP," The Employee Stock Ownership Association Profile Series (Washington, D.C.: ESOP Association, no date).

9. Robert Strickland, "Testimony to the United States Committee on Finance."

Chapter 14

1. "A Co-op Restaurant: All from Scratch," *New York Times*, December 7, 1983.

2. National Center for Employee Ownership, *Common Ground Restaurant Case Study and Interviews* (Arlington, Va.: NCEO, 1984).

Epilogue

1. These plans, known as PAYSOPs, gave a tax credit for companies to provide a trivial amount of ownership. They were responsible for creating most of the worker-owners in companies less than 15 percent employee owned. The Senate Finance Committee estimates that the PAYSOP accounts for over 90 percent of the annual $2.5 to $3 billion ESOP tax subsidy.

2. Adam Blumenthal, *Steel Stock: Arrangement for Employee Ownership and Participation in the U.S. Steel Industry* (Cambridge, Mass.: Harvard Study Group on Worker Ownership and Participation, 1986); Beverly Smaby, Christopher Meek, Joseph Blasi, and Catherine Barnes, *A Report on Employee Ownership and Participation in Eastern Air Lines, Inc.* (Washington, D.C.: U.S. Department of Labor, Bureau of Labor-Management Cooperation, Research Division, forthcoming).

3. Lynn Williams (President, USWA), Remarks at Industrial Union Department AFL-CIO Executive Council Subcommittee on Pension and Benefit Fund Investment Policy Meeting, Washington, D.C., January 9, 1986.

4. William Foote Whyte and Charles Craypo, *A Report on Worker Buyouts* (Ithaca, N.Y.: Cornell University School of Industrial Labor Relations, 1983).

5. John Hoerr, "Revolution or Ripoff?" *Business Week* (April 15, 1985): 94–108; John Hoerr, "America's Labor Laws Weren't Written for a Global Economy," *Business Week* (January 13, 1986).

6. Joseph R. Blasi, *Employee Ownership and the Transfiguration of the American Labor Law Tradition* (Cambridge, Mass.: Harvard University Study Group on Worker Ownership and Participation in Business, 1984).

7. Douglas Kruse, *Employee Ownership and Employee Attitudes: Two Case Studies* (Norwood, Pa.: Norwood Editions, 1983).

8. Joseph R. Blasi, *The Communal Experience of the Kibbutz* (New Brunswick, N.J.: Transaction Books, 1986).

9. Keith Bradley and Alan Gelb, *Cooperation at Work: The Mondragon Experience* (London: Heinemann Educational Books, 1983).

RESOURCES

The National Center for Employee Ownership (NCEO)
927 South Walter Reed Drive, Suite 1
Arlington, VA 22204
703-979-2375

> NCEO is a private, nonprofit, membership, information, and research corporation. It publishes a bimonthly newsletter, researches employee ownership issues, provides monographs on various aspects of the subject, holds workshops and conferences, and maintains a referral service. Membership in the center is $25 for individuals, $60 for companies and organizations. Included in the center's publication list are: an introductory reader; a model ESOP; a guide to unions and employee ownership; a clipping service; a research review; case studies; and a guide to federal and state legislation. Write for a free catalogue.

Action Resources West
1218 South 1200 West
Salt Lake City, Utah 84104
801-378-2664

> Consulting on workplace participation programs, especially in employee ownership settings. Contact Warner Woodworth or Chris Meek.

Center for Community Self-Help
P.O. Box 3259
Durham, NC 27005
919-683-3019

Technical assistance for employee buyout efforts, cooperatives, and other matters related to plant closing and worker ownership in the North Carolina area. Operates credit union and loan fund to assist employee ownership efforts. Contact Martin Eakes.

Industrial Cooperative Association
58 Day Street
Somerville, MA 02144
617-629-2700

Technical assistance, information and loan fund for worker cooperatives, democratic ESOPs, employee buyouts, and community development. Contact Steve Dawson.

Michigan Employee Ownership Center
1880 Penobscot Building
Detroit, MI 48226
313-964-2460

Nonprofit local support group focusing on assistance to unions and small businesses. Contact Deborah Groban Olson.

New York Interface
666 Broadway, Suite 800
New York, New York 10012
212-674-2121

Research, workshops, and technical assistance for employee ownership in the New York area. Contact Marilyn Ondrasik.

Philadelphia Association for Cooperative Enterprise
133 S. 18th Street, 3rd Floor
Philadelphia, PA 19107
215-561-7079

Technical assistance for employee ownership, focusing on cooperatives and employee buyouts. Contact Sherman Kreiner.

Program for Employment and Workplace Systems
School of Industrial and Labor Relations
Box 1000, Ives Hall
Cornell University
Ithaca, NY 14853
202-256-4530

Organizational assistance and research on employee ownership and labor-management cooperation programs. Contact William Foote Whyte.

Social Economy Program
Department of Sociology
Boston College
Chestnut Hill, MA 02167
617-969-0100, ext. 4048

Newsletter on workplace democracy and related topics; graduate education in workplace democracy, employee ownership, and related topics. Contact Charles Derber.

Study Group on Worker Ownership and Participation
10 Divinity Lane
Harvard University
Cambridge, MA 02138

Research and speakers series on employee ownership. Contact Joseph Blasi.

Twin Streams Educational Center
243 Flemington Street
Chapel Hill, NC 27514
919-929-3316

Educational programs for workers in employee ownership efforts. Contact Wes Hare.

Utah State University Business and Economic Development
Services
UMC 35, POB 95923
Logan, Utah 84322
801-750-2283

> Research and information on plant closings, employee own-
> ership, and related issues. Contact Gary Hansen.

Work Books
POB 587
Gatesville, NC 27938
919-357-1910

> Books on employee ownership, workplace democracy and
> related topics. Contact Frank Adams.

BIBLIOGRAPHY

Adams, Frank. *Making Production, Making Democracy: A Case Study of Teaching in the Workplace.* Chapel Hill, N.C.: Twin Stream Educational Center. 1982.

Arzensek, Vlado. "Problems of Yugoslav Self-Management." In Colin Crouch and Frank A. Heller, eds., *Organizational Democracy and Political Processes.* New York: Wiley, 1983.

Barnes, Peter. *Reflections of a Socialist Entrepreneur.* Arlington, Va.: National Center for Employee Ownership, 1983. (Unpublished.)

Berle, Adolph, and Gardina Means. *The Modern Corporation and Private Property.* New York: Macmillan, 1933.

Berman, Katrina. "The Worker Owned Plywood Companies." In Joyce Rothschild-Whitt and Frank Lindenfield, eds., *Workplace Democracy and Social Change,* pp. 161–76. Boston: Porter-Sargent, 1982.

Blasi, Joseph R. *The Communal Experience of the Kibbutz.* New Brunswick, N.J.: Transaction Books, 1986.

———. *Employee Ownership and the Transfiguration of the American Labor Law Tradition.* Cambridge, Mass.: Harvard University Study Group on Worker Ownership and Participation in Business, 1984.

Bloom, David, and Jane T. Trahan. *Customized Fringe Benefits.* Work in America Institute Studies in Productivity. New York: Pergamon Press, forthcoming.

Bloom, Steven. *Employee Ownership and Firm Performance.* Cambridge, Mass.: Harvard University Study Group on Worker Ownership and Participation in Business, 1985.

Blumenthal, Adam. *Steel Stock: Arrangements for Employee*

Ownership and Participation in the U.S. Steel Industry. Cambridge, Mass.: Harvard University Study Group on Worker Ownership and Participation in Business, 1986.

Bradley, Keith, and Alan Gelb. *Cooperation at Work: The Mondragon Experience.* London: Heinemann Educatioal Books, 1983.

Campbell, Megan. "Case Study: The M. W. Carr Company." *Employee Ownership* 1, no. 3 (December 1981): 2–3.

Cavanaugh, Richard. *The Winning Peformance of America's Mid-Sized Companies.* Chicago: McKenzie, 1983.

Conte, Michael, and Arnole Tannenbaum. *Employee Ownership.* Ann Arbor: Survey Research Center, University of Michigan, 1980.

"A Co-op Restaurant: All from Scratch." *New York Times.* December 7, 1983.

"Coops Turn to Catholics." *San Francisco Examiner.* September 2, 1984, p. A1.

Ellerman, David. *The Democratic ESOP.* Somerville, Mass.: Industrial Cooperative Association, 1985.

ESOP Association of America. "The Allied Plywood ESOP." The Employee Stock Ownership Association Profile Series. Berkeley: ESOP Association of America, no date.

––––––. "The Lowe's Companies ESOP." The Employee Stock Ownership Association Profile Series. Berkeley: ESOP Association of America, no date.

––––––. "The Up-Right ESOP." The Employee Stock Ownership Association Profile Series. Berkeley: ESOP Association of America, no date.

"ESOP—Remunerative Road to Productivity." *Building Supply News* (March 1982).

"ESOPs of the Home Improvement Industry." *Building Supply News* (August 1982), 113–17.

Finegold, David Louis. *Quality of Work Life at ATT.* Cambridge, Mass.: Harvard University Study Group on Worker Ownership and Participation in Business, 1984.

Ford, Ramona L. "The Phillips Paper Corporation: A Case Study of an Employee Stock Purchase, Stock Bonus, Profit-Sharing, and Employee Job Committee Plan." South Texas State University, February 1983. (Unpublished.)

Freund, William C., and Eugene Epstein, *People and Productivity: The New York Stock Exchange Guide to Financial Incentives and the Quality of Work Life.* Homewood, Ill.: Dow Jones-Irwin, 1984.

Guest, Robert H. *Innovative Work Practices.* Work in America Institute Studies in Productivity, Number 21. New York: Pergamon Press, 1982.

Hecksher, Charles. *Democracy at Work: In Whose Interests?* Ph.D. dissertation, Harvard University Department of Sociology, 1981.

Hoerr, John. "America's Labor Laws Weren't Written for a Global Economy." *Business Week* (January 13, 1986).

―――. "Revolution or Ripoff?" *Business Week* (April 15, 1985).

Kelso, Louis, and Patricia Hetter. *Two-Factor Theory: The Economics of Reality.* New York: Vintage, 1967.

Klein, Katherine, and Corey Rosen. "Job Generation Performance of Employee Owned Companies." *Monthly Labor Review* 106, no. 8 (August 1983): 15–19.

Kruse, Douglas. *Employee Ownership and Employee Attitudes: Two Case Studies.* Norwood, Penn.: Norwood Editions, 1983.

"Lowe's Companies." *Fortune.* December 1972.

Lowe's Company. *Annual Report: 1977.* North Wilkesboro, N.C.: Lowe's Company. 1977.

"Lowe's Is Shooting for a Bigger League." *Building Supply News* (January 1983).

"Lowe's Knows How to Communicate." *San Francisco Chronicle.* July 15, 1978.

"Lowe's Largesse." *Newsweek.* March 31, 1975.

Marsh, Thomas, and Dale McAllister. "ESOP's Tables." *Journal of Corporation Law* no. 3 (Spring 1981): 613–17.

Miller, Marc. "Workers' Owned." *Southern Exposure* (Winter 1980).

National Center for Employee Ownership (NCEO). *Allied Plywood Case Study and Interviews.* Arlington, Va.: NCEO, 1982.

———. *Common Ground Restaurant Case Study and Interviews.* Arlington, VA.: NCEO, 1984.

———. *Evaluation Research Corporation Case Study and Interviews.* Arlington, Va.: NCEO, 1982.

———. *Fastener Industries Case Study and Interviews.* Arlington, Va.: NCEO, 1983.

———. *Freewheel Bicycle Case Study and Interviews.* Arlington, Va.: NCEO, 1984.

———. *Hyatt-Clark Industries Case Study and Interviews.* Arlington, Va.: NCEO, 1983.

———. *The Lowe's Companies Case Study and Interviews.* Arlington, Va.: NCEO, 1983.

———. *M. W. Carr Case Study and Interviews.* Arlington, Va.: NCEO, 1981.

———. *M. W. Carr Case Study and Interviews.* Arlington, Va.: NCEO, 1983.

———. *Phillips Paper Corporation Case Study and Interviews.* Arlington, Va.: NCEO, 1983.

———. *Quad/Graphics Case Study and Interviews.* Arlington, Va.: NCEO, 1984.

———. *Up-Right, Inc. Case Study and Interviews.* Arlington, Va.: NCEO, 1983.

New York Stock Exchange. *People and Productivity: A Challenge to Corporate America.* New York: Office of Economic Research, New York Stock Exchange, 1982.

Olson, Deborah Groban. "Union Experience with Worker Ownership." *Wisconsin Law Review* 5 (1982).

Patard, Richard. "Employee Ownership in the 1920's." 1982 (Unpublished.)

Quad/Graphics, Inc. *Quad/Graphics Annual Report: 1983.* Pewaukee, Wis.: Quad/Graphics, 1983.

———. *Quad/Graphics Annual Report: 1984.* Pewaukee, Wis.: Quad/Graphics, 1984.

Rosen, Corey; Katherine Klein; and Karen Young. *Employee*

Ownership in America: The Equity Solution. Lexington, Mass.: Lexington Books, 1986.

Rosen, Corey, and Jonathan Feldman. "Employee Benefits in Employee Stock Ownership Plans." *Pension World* 22, no. 2 (February 1986): 34–39.

Rus, Veljoko. "Yugoslav Self-Management—30 Years Later." In Bernhard Wilpert and Arnot Surge, eds., *Perspectives on Organizational Democracy.* New York: Wiley, 1984.

Smaby, Beverly; Christopher Meek; Joseph Blasi; and Catherine Barnes. *A Report on Employee Ownership and Participation in Eastern Air Lines, Inc.* Washington, D.C.: U.S. Department of Labor, Bureau of Labor-Management Cooperation, Research Division, forthcoming.

Storch, Sergio. "M. W. Carr." 1983. (Unpublished.)

Strickland, Robert. "The Lowe's ESOP." Presentation at the Second Annual ESOP Symposium. Georgetown University Law School, Washington, D.C., September 25, 1980.

————. "Testimony to the United States Senate Committee on Finance." May 19, 1981.

Tannenbaum, Arnold; Harold Cook; and Jack Lohman. *The Relationship of Employee Ownership to the Technological Adaptiveness and Performance of Companies.* Report to the National Science Foundation. Ann Arbor: University of Michigan Institute for Social Research, 1984.

U.S. General Accounting Office. "Initial Results of a Survey on Employee Stock Ownership Plans." Washington, D.C.: GAO-PEMD-85-11, 1985.

Up-Right, Inc. "Up-Right Employee Stock Ownership Plan Handbook." Berkeley: ESOP Association of America, 1975.

Wagner, Ira. "Employee Ownership in Corporate America." Report to the New York Stock Exchange. Arlington, Va.: National Center for Employee Ownership, 1984.

Weinberg, Edgar. *Labor-Management Cooperation for Productivity.* Work in America Institute Studies in Productivity, Number 35. New York: Pergamon, 1983.

Weitzman, Martin L. *The Share Economy.* Cambridge, Mass.: Harvard University Press, 1984.

169

Whyte, William Foote, and Charles Craypo. *A Report on Worker Buyouts.* Ithaca, N.Y.: Cornell University School of Industrial Labor Relations, 1986.

Williams, Frank, and Laurie Kellog. "Cut and Sew—Coop Style." Somerville, Mass.: Industrial Cooperative Association, September 1983.

"The Workers' Company." *Boston Globe.* September 3, 1981.

"Workers Team Up to Tough It Out on Their Own." *News and Observer* (Raleigh, N.C.). April 17, 1984.

"Workers' Owned Sewing Company." *Industrial Cooperative Association Bulletin.* Somerville, Mass, March 1984.

Wojahn, Ellen. "Management by Walking Away." *Inc.* (October 1983): 68–76.

INDEX

ABOUT THE AUTHORS

Michael Quarrey is projects director of the National Center for Employee Ownership. The Center is a private, nonprofit membership research and information organization located in Arlington, Virginia. Before joining the Center in 1984 he worked as a systems analyst for Senator Paul Tsongas, for the Social Service Planning Corporation, and for Kennedy Die Castings, Inc. He received an M.S. from Dartmouth's Resource Policy Center in 1986 and a B.S. from Worcester Polytechnic Institute in 1983.

Joseph Blasi teaches social studies at Harvard University, where he has taught since 1977. He also leads a study group on worker ownership and participation in business at Harvard, is working on a Labor Department contract examining the Eastern Air Lines case, and is a member of the board of directors of the National Center for Employee Ownership. He has been studying worker ownership and participation in management for over a decade in Israel's kibbutz communities and trade union sector, the United States, and Europe. From 1976 to 1981 Blasi served as an adviser on employee ownership legislation in the U.S. House of Representatives. He has published extensively on worker ownership and participation in management.

Corey Rosen is the cofounder and executive director of the National Center for Employee Ownership. Prior to cofounding the Center he was a professional staff member in the U.S. Senate and an assistant professor of politics at Ripon College. He received a Ph.D. from Cornell University in 1973 and a B.A. from Wesleyan University in 1970. He has written over fifty articles on employee ownership for various business, professional, and academic publications and is the coauthor of *Employee Ownership in America: The Equity Solution.*